BEST OF

Beijing

Korina Miller

Contents

Best of Beijing
1st edition – March 2004

Published by Lonely Planet Publications Pty Ltd
ABN 36 005 607 983
www.lonelyplanet.com or AOL keyword: lp

Lonely Planet offices
Australia Locked Bag 1, Footscray, Vic 3011
☎ 03 8379 8000 fax 03 8379 8111
talk2us@lonelyplanet.com.au
USA 150 Linden St, Oakland, CA 94607
☎ 510 893 8555 Toll Free 800 275 8555
fax 510 893 8572
info@lonelyplanet.com
UK 72-82 Rosebery Avenue, London EC1R 4RW
☎ 020 7841 9000 fax 020 7841 9001
go@lonelyplanet.co.uk
France 1 rue du Dahomey, 75011 Paris
☎ 01 55 25 33 00 fax 01 55 25 33 01
bip@lonelyplanet.fr
www.lonelyplanet.fr

Designers Sally Darmody & Gerilyn Attebery **Editor**
Carolyn Boicos **Proofer** Cherry Prior **Cartographers** Adrian
Persoglia & Karen Fry **Cover Designer** Gerilyn Attebery
Project Managers Celia Wood & Charles Rawlings-Way
Commissioning Editor Michael Day **Series Designer**
Gerilyn Attebery **Series Publishing Manager** Katrina
Browning **Regional Publishing Manager** Virginia Maxwell

Special Thanks to Björn Wiesler, who updated parts of
this book during production

Photographs
Photography by Phil Weymouth. Other photos by Neil
Setchfield (p47) & Keren Su/China Span (p91).

Many of the images in this guide are available for
licensing from Lonely Planet Images:
www.lonelyplanetimages.com

Front cover photograph
Cleaner sweeps steps inside the Forbidden City
(Phil Weymouth)

ISBN 1 74059 386 3

READER FEEDBACK

Things change – prices go up, schedules change, good places go bad and bad places improve or go bankrupt. So, if you find things better or worse, recently opened or long since closed, please tell us and help make the next edition even more accurate. Send all correspondence to the Lonely Planet office closest to you (listed on page 2) or visit www.lonelyplanet.com/feedback.

Lonely Planet books provide independent advice. Lonely Planet does not accept advertising in guidebooks, nor payment in exchange for listing or endorsing any place or business. Lonely Planet writers do not accept discounts or payments in exchange for positive coverage of any sort.

From the Publisher

AUTHOR

Korina Miller

Korina lived the first 18 years of her life on Vancouver Island. Since then, she hasn't lived in any one place for very long, managing to take in parts of Japan, India, Egypt, Europe, the South Pacific and South and Central America. Along the way she picked up a degree in Communications & Canadian Studies and an MA in Migration Studies from Sussex University. She spent six months in Shanghai and Yunnan, researching cooperatives and ecotourism for the David See-Chai Lam Centre for International Communications. Her travels in China have taken her from the Manchurian border in the north to the Tibetan Plateau in the southwest. She is co-author of LP's *China* and *South-West China*.

Thank you to Paul, the perfect travelling partner, to Mum and Dad for the home comforts, to Michael and Carolyn for their support, to Moggy for the info, to Meghan for the typing help, to fellow travellers for their tips and to the people of Beijing for their kindness and enthusiasm.

PHOTOGRAPHER

Phil Weymouth

Phil's family moved from Australia to Iran in the late 1960s and called Tehran home until the revolution in 1979. Phil studied photography in Melbourne and returned to the Middle East to work as a photographer in Bahrain for several years. He then spent a decade working with an Australian rural media company. Currently he runs a freelance photojournalism business based in Melbourne, working for a variety of Australian and international media and publishing companies. He continues to travel extensively, supplying images to Lonely Planet Images, writing stories and avoiding his office.

How to Use This Book

SYMBOLS

☎	telephone
✉	address
🖳	email/website address
$	admission
☾	opening hours
ⓘ	information
Ⓜ	metro
🚌	bus
♿	wheelchair access
🍴	on site/nearby eatery
👶	child-friendly venue
Ⓥ	good vegetarian selection

COLOUR-CODING

Each chapter has a different colour code, which is reflected on the maps for quick reference (eg all Highlights are bright yellow on the maps).

MAPS

The fold-out maps inside the front and back covers are numbered from 1 to 7. All sights and venues in the text have map references which indicate where to find them on the maps; eg (4, G7) means Map 4, grid reference G7.

PRICES

Price gradings (eg Y10/5) usually indicate adult/concession entry charges to a venue. Concession prices can include senior, student, member or coupon discounts.

Introducing Beijing

Visiting Beijing is like attending a giant Chinese banquet: big, bright, bold and there's never a dull moment. On one side of you sits old Beijing, wise and calm, with a mesmerising history. On the other side of you sits a chic and worldly Beijing, busy making a shopping date on a mobile phone. The main room is opulent and explosively loud; but if you head down into the narrow corridors you'll find retired workmen silently meditating over their next move on the mah jong table, and old women practising their fan dancing to hushed Chinese pop music. The entertainment is magnetic, the food is fantastic and there's so much tea you could swim in it.

Beijing is a city of contrasts. China's most ancient and dazzling sights sit in unruffled splendour next to traffic-riddled freeways and state-of-the-art high-rises. Department stores filled to the gills with European designer fashions back onto *hutongs*, Beijing's ancient and vibrant alleyways.

With the 2008 Olympics on the slow boat to China, the city is getting a major scrub and makeover: improved transport, more and better services and maybe even cleaner air are on the way. If you're a sightseer, a shopper, a kite fanatic, a kung fu fan, an architect, an opera enthusiast, a hiker, a biker or you just love food, Beijing is a perfect destination.

Cycling in the fast lane

Highlights

Try as hard as you like – it's impossible not to be wowed by Beijing's gob-smacking sights. Even the most blasé tourists find themselves entering into scrums in order to get to the front of the queues at the Forbidden City. The most weathered travellers still get a buzz from climbing up Tiananmen Gate for a Mao-esque perspective of the vast, history-soaked square. Not all of Beijing's sights are overrun with tourists and many of the lesser-known must-sees offer a breath of serenity in the midst of the buzzing city.

At all but the quietest sights, water, snacks and souvenirs are for sale in and around the grounds, although vendors inside often charge up to double the going street price. Children under 1.2m often get into sights free or receive a substantial discount, as do students and seniors. If you're planning to take in a number of sights, the Beijing Museum Ticket Card (Y80) is very worthwhile: it includes entrance to 60 sights, including Prince Gong's Residence, the Ancient Observatory, the Great Wall at Badaling and the China Millennium Monument. The ticket is available at Wangfujing subway station (Oriental Plaza exit) and from participating museums.

STOPPING OVER?

One Day Mingle in Tiananmen Square and have your photo taken at the top of Tiananmen Gate. Lose yourself in the Forbidden City before wandering up through Jingshan Park for a sunset view of the City's golden rooftops. Dine at The Courtyard, where you can visit a gallery and linger in the cigar lounge.

Two Days As for one day, but also take in the Summer Palace. Hop in a rickshaw near Prince Gong's for a tour of Beijing's *hutongs* (alley-ways). Dine at the Sichuan Fandian and then relax at one of the bars or cafés along Qianhai Lake.

Three Days As for two days, then visit Lama Temple. Spend the afternoon shopping along Dazhalan Jie and Liulichang Jie. Later, enjoy a traditional opera at Zhengyi Ci Theatre.

Lowlights
- The Beijing Zoo with its miniscule cells and depressed inmates
- Hordes of tourists with sharpened elbows clawing their way to the front of queues
- Witnessing spitting like you've never seen or heard before
- Struggling to squeeze onto an overflowing, dilapidated local bus

TIANANMEN 天安门 (4, H7)

Step inside the heart of China. Tiananmen (Gate of Heavenly Peace) is both the symbolic and political epicentre of China. While the cement plain of Tiananmen Square (p33) is the people's stage, the gate is the podium of the powerful. Built in the 15th century and restored in the 17th, imperial royalty and communist leaders alike have used Tiananmen as a rostrum for viewing troops and for proclaiming the law of the land to assembled crowds. It was here that Mao declared the founding of the People's Republic on 1 October 1949 and, throughout his life under the political limelight, he ruled the roost from this vantage.

Seven parallel bridges lead over a stream to the gate's five doors. In imperial days, the centre bridge and door could only be used by the emperor. Since the arrival of the Communist Party, this door has been crowned with an enormous portrait of Mao. To the helmsman's left is written 'Long

INFORMATION

- ✉ Tiananmen Dong
- ☎ 6524 3322
- Ⓜ Tiananmen Dong
- 🕐 8.30am-4.30pm
- 💲 Y15; compulsory bag check Y3-5
- ♿ excellent
- 🍴 Wangfujing Snack Street (p72)

Even men in uniform can't resist a photo op

Crackin' Portrait

Staring down at you from Tiananmen, Mao's formidable gaze makes the hair rise on the back of your neck. This gigantic portrait, moles and all, symbolises the power and might of the Communist Party. During the pro-democratic demonstrations of 1989, workers from Mao's home province of Hunan mercilessly pelted the commander with paint-filled eggs. Luckily, the Party has a number of spare portraits hidden away and, before you could say 'Big Brother', the splattered original was replaced.

Live the People's Republic of China' and to his right, 'Long Live the Unity of the Peoples of the World'.

A visit to Tiananmen is your chance to see the gate from the inside and to savour the vista of the world's largest square. Directly ahead of you, Mao rests in his **mausoleum** (p37), with the regal **Qianmen** (p30) beyond. To the west is the **Chinese Revolution & History Museum** (p26) and to the east lurks the **Great Hall of the People** (p29).

FORBIDDEN CITY 紫禁城 (7)

For 500 years the walls of the Forbidden City drew an impenetrable line between the imperial household and the general population. Exceptionally well preserved, the palace was first opened to the public in 1949, allowing visitors to step into a world of emperors, eunuchs, ceremony and splendour.

INFORMATION

- ✉ Tiananmen Dong, through Tiananmen Gate
- ☎ 6513 2255
- Ⓜ Tiananmen Dong or Tiananmen Xi
- ☽ Apr–mid-Oct 8.30am-5pm, mid-Oct–Mar 8.30am-4.30pm
- $ Apr-Oct Y60; Nov-Mar Y40; kids under 1.2m free
- ⓘ audio tour by Roger Moore Y40, plus ID card deposit; guided tours at the entrance
- ✕ Purple Vine Teahouse (p83); The Courtyard (p70)

The majestic northwest tower

The palace was originally established by Emperor Yongle (via a million labourers) between 1406 and 1420. In order to show his power and wealth and yet 'humbly' accept his natural inferiority to the gods, the palace has a mere 9999.5 rooms, half a room less than the Jade Emperor's heavenly palace. With 800 buildings covering 720,000 sq m, the palace is so large that a full-time restoration squad is continuously repainting and repairing. It's estimated to take 10 years to do a full renovation.

The buildings you see today are mainly post-18th century. Fire has always been a threat to the wooden palace, with six major and countless minor blazes sending buildings up in smoke. Many fires were the result of fireworks displays gone awry or wayward lanterns. Invading Manchus burned the palace to the ground in 1644 and eunuchs torched a number of buildings in 1923 in an attempt to cover up their looting of palace treasures. Imperial guards fought the blazes with water stored in huge vats, many of which still dot the palace grounds.

Fourteen Ming emperors and 10 Qing emperors called the Forbidden City home. Many became absorbed in the splendour of life inside the palace, to the detriment of their rule and the living conditions outside. Often emperors would hand over the dull task of ruling to the court eunuchs in order to take up the more interesting hobbies of collecting concubines or writing poetry.

The **Hall of Supreme Harmony** is the largest structure in the palace grounds, used for occasions such as the emperor's birthday, and coronations. The hall is decorated with 13,844 dragons.

In front of the hall is a sundial and standard measuring container, alluding to the emperor's mastery of both time and space. Also in front of the hall is a bronze turtle, symbolising longevity and stability. Inside the hall, the throne is guarded by two *luduan* (mythical beasts believed to understand all languages and able to cover 9000 leagues of distance in a day).

The **Palace of Heavenly Purity** was the living quarters of the

Slip-Not
In the belief that frequent sex with young girls could sustain one's youth (a belief also subscribed to by Mao Zedong), emperors would keep large numbers of imperial concubines. Emperor Jiajiang of the Ming dynasty kept over 1000 and his treatment of these women was notoriously cruel; over 200 died of ill treatment.

Unwilling to put up with this brutality any longer, 16 concubines attempted to strangle Jiajiang while he slept. Discovering that the incorrectly tied rope wouldn't tighten, a hairpin was brandished. This might have done the trick had the empress not wandered in and saved her unconscious husband. The 16 concubines were dismembered; a death believed to exclude them from the next life.

emperors. This building contained nine bedrooms, each with three beds. To safeguard against attack while he slept, the emperor would retire to a different bed each night. Further north, the elaborate **Palace of Earthly Tranquillity** was the sleeping quarters of the Ming empresses; during the Qing dynasty, it was used for only three days of each reign as the nuptial chamber.

LAMA TEMPLE 雍和宫 (4, A9)

Beijing's most colourful temple is overflowing with tapestries, frescoes, statuary, plumes of incense smoke and prostrate worshippers. The immaculately maintained buildings are an architectural feat and it is easy to understand why this is one of Beijing's most popular sights.

INFORMATION

- ✉ 12 Yonghegong Dajie
- ☎ 6404 4499
- Ⓜ Yonghegong
- 🕑 9am–4pm
- 💲 Y25
- ⓘ audio guide Y20/10 English/Chinese; guided tours at the front gate
- ✕ Mao's Family Restaurant (p71)

Honey, I shrunk the shrine!

Fancy living in a place like this? Count Yin Zhen did – until he became Emperor Yongzheng and packed his bags for the Forbidden City. His former residence became Yonghe Palace until 1744 when it was converted into Lama Temple, a lamasery for legions of Mongolian and Tibetan monks. Today it remains one of the most renowned Tibetan Buddhist temples outside of Tibet.

When Yongzheng's successor, Emperor Qianlong, came to power, Lama Temple took on new significance. A Buddhist, Qianlong claimed to be sympathetic to followers of the religion but, in actuality, directed his energies into pacifying the discontented Mongolians and Tibetans by 'training' (and controlling) their Lamas at Lama Temple.

Nevertheless, the temple had a ghoulish reputation for supposedly harbouring the more sinister aspects of Tibetan Buddhism, such as human sacrifice. When photographer James Ricalton visited in the late 19th century, he noted: '…it is one of the most dirty, dingy, smoky, ramshackle establishments in the whole world and filled with one thousand five hundred Mongolian and Tibetan ignorant fanatics, called priests.'

In 1792 Qianlong further extended his minority control by instituting a new system for choosing Buddhist leaders that was not unlike a rigged lottery. Possible names were chosen in consultation with Qianlong and placed in two golden vases. One was taken to Lhasa to draw the Dalai Lama's name and the other remained at Lama Temple to draw the Panchen Lama.

The lamasery has five halls, each one taller and more impressive than the previous. They are designed and decorated in a mosaic of styles – Mongolian, Tibetan and Han – and are surrounded by courtyards and galleries. The lamasery's erotic statuary of intertwining gods and humans were once used to educate emperors' sons in the more pleasurable facts of life. Today they are draped in yellow cloth so as not to corrupt your gaze.

DON'T MISS
- The intricate mandala sand painting in Falun Dian Hall, made entirely of natural colouring
- The altar of the 6th Panchen Lama, kept in the western exhibition hall
- The pair of regal lions guarding the lamasery

The most Tibetan-styled building is **Falun Dian**, the fourth hall, which is used for study and prayer. Here you'll find a large bronze statue of Tsong Khapa (1357-1419), founder of the Gelukpa (Yellow Hat sect), and frescoes depicting his life.

In the last hall, **Wanfu Ge**, you have to crick your neck to take in the astounding 26m-high Maitreya Buddha. Believe it or not (and the *Guinness Book of World Records* did, as certified on a plaque outside), the statue is carved from a single block of sandalwood. The pungent smoke curling up from the yak-butter lamps reminds you that the wood originates in Tibet.

At the rear of the lamasery are two exhibition halls. Inside the western one are relics from the Tibet-China relationship and in the eastern hall is an introduction to the genealogy of the Dalai Lama and photos depicting the activities of today's lamas. While both halls are intriguing, the eastern one is lacking in English explanations and the information displayed in both halls should definitely be taken with a bucket of salt.

Worshipping at the altar, Lama Temple

SUMMER PALACE 颐和园 (5)

The playground of the royal court, these enormous grounds were where the imperial family and entourage came to escape the interminable heat of the city. A day can easily be spent here taking in the sights, strolling along tree-lined paths and floating in a paddleboat on Kunming Lake.

INFORMATION

- ✉ Yiheyuan Lu, Haidian District
- ☎ 6288 1144
- Ⓜ Xixhimen, then bus 375 or taxi
- 🚌 303, 346, 808 or 826 from Qianmen area
- 🕐 7am-5pm
- 💲 Y20-30/10; incl all sights Y40-50/20
- ⓘ audio guides Y30

Long a royal garden, the grounds were embellished and expanded by Emperor Qianlong in the 18th century. In 1860 many of the buildings were severely damaged during the Second Opium War. Eighteen years later, Empress Dowager Cixi began a refit. She used money earmarked for a modern navy and, perhaps in honour of this, spent a large chunk of it on a huge, tasteless **marble boat**. You'll find it in the northeast of Kunming Lake. The Summer Palace was razed and neglected a few more times, prompting a string of further restorations.

The main entrance to the Palace is in the east of the grounds. Just inside this gate is the **Hall of Benevolence and Longevity**, the chief palace structure where the emperor handled state affairs and received envoys. Among the bronze animals in front of the hall is the mythical *qilin* (Chinese unicorn). Nearby is the **Garden of Virtue and Harmony** (Y5), where you can see traditional costumes and props.

Nature's detail on a garden wall

Sit back, relax and watch the waters of Kunming Lake flow past Mirror Bridge

To the north, the artificial **Longevity Hill** contains the majority of the park's interesting buildings. **Cloud Dispensing Hall** was one of the few structures to escape the attention of Anglo-French forces, and the impressive **Tower of Fragrant Buddha** (Y10) offers fabulous views across the lake. The **Long Corridor**, which runs for over 700m along the northern shore of Kunming Lake, is painted with countless mythical scenes.

In the west of the grounds, an excellent walk spans the lake across **Jade Belt Bridge**, **Mirror Bridge**, **Chain Bridge** and **Willow Bridge**. Three-quarters of the palace grounds are consumed by Kunming Lake. You can take a ferry across it (9am-4pm; Y5), cruise on a pleasure boat around it (9am-4pm; Y6) or paddle on it (8am-4.30pm; Y40/hr, deposit Y200).

In the very north of the complex is **Suzhou Street** (Y10). Originally exclusive to the emperor and his entourage, the shopping street has been rebuilt in classic Ming style, and its stalls are once again open for business. All purchases must be made with antique Ming coins; exchange your Renminbi at the top of the street.

Dragon Woman

Like many other Qing-dynasty teenagers, at the age of 15 Cixi gave up her true love to become one of Emperor Xianfeng's concubines. Her cunningness and intelligence soon made her a favourite of the Emperor, particularly after she gave birth to his only son in 1856. Cixi's subsequent rise to power was largely due to the convenient deaths of her adversaries. Xianfeng died at the age of 30 and his empress followed suit a few years later. This made Cixi's five-year-old son, Tongzhi, the new emperor, and Cixi herself the ruling Dowager Empress.

Cixi held the government reins for over 40 years in total, galloping over anyone who got in her way – including her own son. Other opponents were slowly starved, thrown down wells or locked away. She spent her reign focusing on her own position rather than the country's; at the end of her life she left nine storerooms of personal treasures, a refurbished Summer Palace, and the Qing dynasty in an irreparable state of decline.

TEMPLE OF HEAVEN 公园 (6)

More park than temple and fairly overrun with tour groups, the Temple of Heaven (Tiantan) is well worth a visit for its exceptional and unique Ming buildings. This sight has become a symbol of Beijing, decorating tourist

INFORMATION

- ✉ Tiantan Donglu
- ☎ 6702 8866
- Ⓜ Qianmen, then bus 120 or taxi
- 🕙 8am-5pm
- 💲 park Y10/15 low/high season; incl all sights Y30/35
- ℹ️ audio guide (from the south entrance) Y20
- ✕ Old Beijing Zhajiang Noodle King (north entrance; p69)

literature and loaning its name to products ranging from tiger balm to plumbing fixtures.

The temple was built in 1420 as a vast stage for the solemn rites performed by the Son of Heaven (aka Emperor), who came here to pray for good harvests, to seek divine approval and to atone for the sins of the people. Similar ceremonies were performed as early as 2600BC and remained an important part of imperial life through to the early 20th century.

The most significant ceremony took place just before the winter solstice, when the emperor and his enormous entourage of elephant chariots, horses, lancers, musicians and 2000 ministers made their way, in total silence, from the Forbidden City to the temple.

The emperor was purified in the **Hall of Abstinence** by fasting from meat, alcohol, women, music and work. He then made sacrifices to the gods and reported to them on the events of the previous years. He would return a month later to beseech the heavens for good luck, especially with the coming year's harvest. As this ceremony was believed to decide the nation's future, any hitch in the proceedings was regarded as a bad omen.

Visitors enjoy the heavenly temple grounds

The temple complex is built for the view of the gods. Seen from above, the temples themselves are round and their bases square, a pattern deriving from the ancient Chinese belief that heaven is round and earth is square. The shape of the 267-hectare park also reflects this, with the northern end a semicircle and the southern end a square.

Beginning in the south, the architecture of the **Round Altar** is based on the imperial number nine and multiples of nine.

Just northeast of here, **Echo Wall** is a perfect half-circle, so a whisper at one end is carried around to the other side. Your chances of experiencing this are slight, however, given the hundreds of tourists attempting to have their 'whispers' heard.

Also in this courtyard are the **Triple-Sounds Stones**; clap your hands while standing on them and listen for the echo once from the first stone, twice from the second and thrice from the third.

Detail on a traditional stove

The octagonal **Imperial Vault of Heaven** at the back of the courtyard is a mini-version of the Hall of Prayer for Good Harvests. It once held the tablets of the emperors' ancestors, used in the winter solstice ceremony.

In the north of the grounds, the round **Hall of Prayer for Good Harvests** is mounted on a three-tiered marble terrace and decorated in blue, yellow and green glazed tiles, representing heaven, earth and the mortal world. Inside, immense pillars symbolise the four seasons and 12 months of the year.

The intricately decorated ceiling is all the more impressive for its lack of nails or cement support. The hall was struck by lightening and burnt to the ground in 1889; it was rebuilt the following year using Oregon fir.

Carved Danbi stone stairway at the Hall of Prayer for Good Harvests

DON'T MISS

- Ringing the giant bell near the Hall of Abstinence
- The sacrificial stove, east of the Gate of Prayer for Good Harvests
- The annex to the west of the Hall of Prayer for Good Harvests

RED GATE GALLERY 红门画廊 (4, J12)

Beneath the giant wooden rafters of the ancient Dongbianmen Watchtower, in a room cooled by vast slate floors, hangs an array of avant-garde art. Established by an Australian art historian, Red Gate Gallery displays Beijing's most innovative and electric modern art. After years of prohibitive restrictions that pushed contemporary work into the corner, the gallery's 15 resident artists are once again stretching their paintbrushes, views and ideas in addressing modern-day issues.

INFORMATION

- ✉ levels 1 & 4, Dongbianmen
- ☎ 6525 1005
- 🖳 www.redgategallery .com
- Ⓜ Beijingzhan
- 🕑 Tues-Sun 10am-5pm
- 💲 free
- ⓘ information sheets at the door

With painting, sculpture, paper-cutting, photography, performance art, lithographs, silkscreen printing and mixed media, the contrast of the modern work in an ancient setting is dramatic, to say the least. With around eight different shows each year, you might also find travelling exhibitions from other parts of China and abroad.

Thinking Art

Think 'Chinese art'. Thinking flowers? A few rocky cliffs? Maybe a bird or two? Chances are, you're not thinking of artists stripping down, wrapping their bodies in linen cloth and pouring bright paints over each other. Neither was anyone in China until Sheng Qi and his colleagues arrived on the scene. Performance art became popular in Beijing in the mid-1980s, but its debut was short, shut down in the oppression that followed the Tiananmen Square crackdown of 1989. Sheng Qi despaired and, as an expression of his anguish, chopped off his little finger and left it buried in a plant pot in Beijing while he fled to Europe to study and perform for a decade. His work in the West soon gained him recognition, particularly his 'Universal Happy Brand Chicken', which saw birds, nudity, drugs, scalpels and urine brought together in an unsavoury way. Sheng Qi is now back in Beijing where his work displayed at the Red Gate Gallery is somewhat more palatable.

Red Gate Gallery: bringing avant-garde art to Beijing

LIULICHANG 琉璃厂 (4, K5)

With gracefully curved tiled roofs, brightly painted doors and cobbled streets, Liulichang exudes a picturesque, old-world atmosphere. The shops lining the streets were once the stomping grounds of the upper-crust Ming and Qing societies; today they are treasure-troves of old coins, lanterns, paper-cuttings, furniture, pottery, swords, books, jade and other objects from days of yore. Visiting them is like stepping back in time.

INFORMATION

- ✉ Liulichang Xijie & Dongjie
- Ⓜ Hepingmen
- ⏱ 10am-6pm
- 💲 free
- 🍴 Tianhai Canting (p69)

West off Nanxinhua Jie, **Rongbaozhai** (19 Liulichang Xijie) has a vast collection of scroll paints, woodblock prints, paper, ink and brushes. Continuing west, the road narrows and takes on a more market-like appearance, with small stalls and tables. This is where you can practise some traditional Chinese bartering.

Heading east from Nanxinhua, you can watch chops being carved

Soft Sell

Perhaps the only thing that has changed along Liulichang is the selling tactics. When historian Harold Acton visited in 1932, he commented:

To visit the antique shops...was like calling at the houses of private collectors who showed one their treasures if the spirit moved them, and otherwise left one to browse... They were content just to drink tea with you and chat about things in general, but in the meantime they were appraising your taste, and if you admired something they thought admirable...immediately you would notice the gleam of enthusiasm in their eyes and a tremulousness in their expressive fingers...

Memoirs of an Aesthete, 1948

in **Xie Xian Shun** (107b Liulichang Dongjie). Carry on to **Yidege** (67 Liulichang Dongjie), where Indian inks have been sold since 1865, and **Daiyuexuan Brush Shop** (73 Liulichang Dongjie), which has provided local artists with top-quality paint brushes since 1916. In the doorways around **Xing Hai Yue Xuan** (97 Liulichang Dongjie) you will often hear melodies being plucked on traditional *yueqins* (guitars) or *guzhengs* (zithers). At the far eastern end of Liulichang, **Beijing Songtangzhai Museum** (p26) is worth a visit.

BEIHAI PARK 北海公园 (4, D5)

The origins of Beihai Park are somewhat mysterious. It was once frequented by emperors looking for a breath of fresh air, but its history tumbles further back to the days of Kublai Khan, who established Beijing as a capital in 1279. Today, all that remains of Khan's palace is a giant, jade wine urn in the Round City near the southern entrance to the park.

INFORMATION

- ✉ Wenjin Jie (south gate); Ping an Dadao (north gate)
- ☎ 6403 1102
- Ⓜ Tiananmen Xi, then bus 5
- ☾ park 6am-8pm; sights 9am-4.45pm
- 💲 park & temples Y5; incl Jade Islet Y10
- ✖ Fangshan Restaurant (p70)

At first glance the park appears to be little more than a lake, however, there is a wealth of sights to take in. Dominating **Jade Islet**, the 36m **White Dagoba** was originally built in 1651 for a visit by the Dalai Lama. The dagoba has since been knocked down twice by earthquakes. The small **Hall of Beneficent Causation**, south of the dagoba, is graced with beautiful glazed Buddha tiles.

The north shore of the park is dotted with temples. The most popular temple complex, **Xitian Fanjing**, houses **Daizhe Hall**, home to three enormous bronze Buddha statues, each with a shock of blue hair. **Jingxinzhai** is worth a visit for its rockeries, painted corridors, restored imperial rooms and the occasional turtle in its ponds.

North West Paradise is the park's most stunning temple. Built by Emperor Qianlong as an offering for his mother's eternal happiness, it is the largest square pavilion in China. Its interior is a carving of the western heavens inhabited by countless Bodhisattvas.

DON'T MISS

- Riding the ferry on North Sea Lake
- Visiting the park in the evening to see older residents playing traditional music, and singing and dancing
- Wang Da Guan's paintings in Kuaixue Hall (p28)

Foxtrotting in the fresh air

DONGYUE TEMPLE 东岳寺 (4, E13)

Surrounded by shopping centres and high-rises, Taoist monks busily attend to the business of the spirit world. With its roots somewhere in the Yuan dynasty, Dongyue Temple is a calm and intriguing retreat.

In the main courtyard of the temple, thousands of small, red, wooden prayer cards have been tied to anything that'll stand still – trees, fences, the front of the temple – and the effect is staggering. Written on each card is a prayer for good fortune, wealth, longevity or bouncing babies. Also in this courtyard is a forest of steles recording the history, beliefs and renovations of the temple over the ages.

Daiyuedian Hall at the back of the temple was first built in 1322 and houses a shrine to the God of Mount Taishan, who is master of 76 departments of heaven, 18 layers of hell and all of the mortal world. You can deposit a coin or two for healthy finances at the **Department for Bestowing Material Happiness**, or pay your respects to feathered friends at the **Department for Flying Birds**. Many of the characters within these departments (particularly those at the **Department for Wandering Souls**) are straight out of a Hollywood horror film.

At the very back of the complex (beginning on the western side) is a fascinating museum. The captions are in Chinese but the photographs and objects tell their own stories of life in old Beijing. If it rains while you're visiting the temple, you're in luck – the **Little Golden Beam** to the west of **Daiyue Palace** will shine with copper specks. Many believe they are gold and that by striding over this slab your wishes will be granted.

Feeling blue? Visit the Department of Urges

INFORMATION

- ✉ Chaoyangmen Wai Dajie
- ☎ 6553 2184
- Ⓜ Chaoyangmen, then bus 110
- ⏱ 9am-4.30pm
- $ Y10/5; kids under 1.2m free
- ✕ Xiheyaju Restaurant (p74)

DON'T MISS

- Bronze Wonder Donkey, the riding animal of God Wen Chang
- The mysterious Daiyuedian Hall
- Trying your luck at bouncing a coin off a bell in the main courtyard

PRINCE GONG'S RESIDENCE 恭王府 (4, C5)

Rockeries, pools of water, elaborately carved gateways, plants, pavilions and corridors are all seamlessly pieced together into one of Beijing's largest private residences. Believed to be the setting of Cao Zueqin's 18th-century classic, *Dream of the Red Mansion*, the palace was bestowed upon Prince Gong by his half-brother, Emperor Xianfeng, in the mid-19th century.

Gong is famous for negotiating with the British during the Second Opium War. With the Summer Palace burned to a crisp, the Forbidden City under threat of a match, and Emperor Xianfeng hiding in Chengde, Gong agreed to all of the Tianjin Treaty terms, including handing over large sums of silver and part of Kowloon to British Hong Kong. In exchange, much of Beijing was left standing and the British supported the Qing against the Taiping Rebellion.

Traditional Chinese gardens are a fusion of nature and architecture, designed to ease, move and aid the mind. The key elements are rocks and water, with every item carefully and purposefully placed. Windows, corridors and rockeries are positioned to enhance or shape your view. For example, as you first enter into this complex, your vision is slightly obscured by a tall rockery; the intention is to break up your view over the entire garden, creating a number of smaller scenes.

In the east of the grounds, the **Grand Opera House** dates back to the Qing dynasty. Unfortunately, unless you're attending an opera (p90), it's rarely open to the public.

This sight is lacking in English translations and those that do exist are cryptic. If you're really keen to know what you're looking at, join a guided tour at the front gate.

INFORMATION

- ✉ 14 Liuyin Jie
- ☎ 6616 8149
- Ⓜ Gulou Dajie, then taxi southwest
- ⏱ 8.30am-4.30pm
- 💲 Y5; kids under 1.2m free
- ⓘ guided tours at the entrance
- ✖ Sichuan Fandian (p72)

Lovely lanterns adorn the corridors

DON'T MISS

- The thousands of brightly coloured carp in Square Pond
- Finding 'happiness' inside the rockery of Terrace for Inviting the Moon
- The more tranquil courtyards in the east of the complex

WHITE CLOUD TEMPLE 白云观 (3, G7)

Long-haired, bearded monks rest in the courtyard while incense sticks as big as bratwurst send clouds of smoke spiralling into the air. You get the distinct impression that little has changed at White Cloud Temple since it was first established in AD739. This was once northern China's centre of Taoism and its huge complex contains countless shrines and courtyards.

Each of the halls is dedicated to a different Taoist official or marshal, from the God protecting Taoism (Wanglingguan) to the God of Wealth. The hall honouring Founder Qi is worth a look for its interior clay walls depicting scenes from the book of Qi.

Southeast of the complex is the **Temple of the God of Thunder**, which houses interesting bronze statues depicting four heavenly generals and the Thunder God himself, in charge of natural disasters, blessings, life and death.

INFORMATION

✉ Baiyun Lu
☎ 6346 3531
Ⓜ Nanlishilu, then walk or taxi 1km
🕘 8.30am-4pm
$ Y10

Chicken's feet: good fortune or good food?

Home-Grown in China

Many say that Taoism is the only 'home-grown' Chinese religion – Buddhism was imported from India and Confucianism is mainly a philosophy. *Dao*, or 'the way', is at the heart of Taoism and is the force behind the universe and all that it holds; it is the inexhaustible spirit of being that can only be experienced through mystical insight. The founder of Taoism (spelled Laotzu, Laotse or Laotze – none of which were his actual name) recorded his beliefs in the 5000 character *Tao Te Ching* (The Way and Its Power), before climbing onto his beast of burden and disappearing down his much sought-after path.

As you enter the temple complex, you pass over a bridge. Beneath it hang two bells; for luck, you can attempt to strike them with old gold coins (you can get some at a nearby stall; Y10 for 50 coins). In the alley outside the temple, vendors sell incense sticks, prayer cards and lots of other Taoist gear.

White Cloud Temple is particularly worth visiting if you're in Beijing over the Spring Festival. During this time the temple fair brings together thousands of worshippers, artisans and street performers.

FRAGRANT HILLS PARK 香山公园 (3, C2)

A part of the Western Hills, this forest retreat is an excellent place for a short jaunt. Within the grounds are beautiful gardens, teahouses and paths. In summer the hill is cloaked in sweet-smelling blossoms; in autumn the maple trees saturate the hills in great splashes of red.

INFORMATION

- ✉ northwest Beijing
- ☎ 6259 1283
- Ⓜ Pinguayuan, then taxi
- ☯ 8am-6pm
- $ Y5
- ✖ Long Hwa Tree Organic Vegetarian Restaurant (p78)

One of the loveliest and most enjoyable ways to reach **Incense Burner Peak** is by cable car (8.30am-5pm; Y30/50 one way/return, children Y10). Follow the excellently maintained, forest-lined trail down (1½hrs). The majority of buildings you pass en route were rebuilt in 1992 and now serve as restaurants and shops.

Near the north gate, **Azure Clouds Temple** (8.30am-4.30pm; Y10) was built in 1331 as a nunnery. Especially worth checking out is the **Hall of Lokapalas**, with its statue of Guanyin surfing through the clouds on a fish. At the back of the temple complex, climb the steps up to **Vayra Throne Pagoda**. Originally built in 1748, it now contains Sun Yatsen's 'Dress Tomb' (ie his hat and clothes). The ex-leader's body was kept here for a couple of years while his mausoleum was being constructed in Nanjing.

Chinese Super Heroes

Two of the first characters you'll come across in Beijing are Heng (Dragon) and Ha (Tiger), temple guardians who fend off evil spirits. Each has a unique combating skill. Heng snorts so fiercely that two glaring white lights appear from his flared nostrils and knock his opponent down. Ha needs only to puff out a breath of yellow smoke to terrorise his opponent out of his wits. Gas mask and goggles, anyone? You'll find Heng and Ha lounging outside Azure Clouds Temple.

Sunday crowds enjoy the fresh air and fragrant parklands

FRAGRANT HILLS BOTANICAL
GARDEN 香山植物园   (3, A3)

A couple of kilometres down the road from Fragrant Hills Park, this is a tranquil place to get lost for a couple of hours, wandering through bamboo, pines and lilac. The 200 hectares of flora and fauna hail from the north, northeast and northwest of China.

The **Beijing Botanical Gardens Conservatory** (8.30am-4pm; Y50/40) is home to over 3000 types of plants from every corner of the globe, including a carnivorous house with Venus flytraps and pitcher plants, a rainforest, desert plants and orchids. In the east of the grounds is a model of **Yellow Leaf Village**, taken from Cao Zueqin's *Dream of the Red Mansion*. Apparently Cao got much of his inspiration for this Qing family saga from this area.

Inside **Wofu Temple** (8am-5pm; Y5) is an enormous reclining effigy of Sakyamuni that is well worth the 15-minute walk from the entrance gate. The Buddha weighs 54 tonnes, is 5.3m from elbow to toe and apparently enslaved 7000 people in its casting during 1321. Above Buddha are the characters *ziai dade*, meaning 'great accomplishment comes from being at ease'. He seems to be taking it literally but, just in case, emperors have given him a number of pairs of gargantuan shoes should he decide to take a stroll. With lotus ponds and the Western Hills in the backdrop, the temple setting is stunning.

INFORMATION
- ✉ northwest Beijing
- Ⓜ Pinguayuan, then taxi
- 🕙 6am-9pm
- 💲 Y4
- ♿ good

DON'T MISS
- The 1300-year-old gingko tree in Penjing Gardens
- Peach blossoms and Magnolia Garden when visiting in spring
- Chrysanthemum Garden and lotuses when visiting in autumn

Sights & Activities

NEIGHBOURHOODS

It's difficult to find a dull neighbourhood in Beijing. The Forbidden City is like a bull's-eye on the Beijing map. Spreading north and northeast from it, **Dongcheng** is where much of the old city survives and where many of Beijing's less-flashy folk live. This is where you'll find many of the former residences of celebrated writers and the imperial clan, as well as a number of temples, with Lama Temple marking the northern boundary of the district. This is the best neighbourhood to ride bikes and explore *hutongs*, especially around the Drum and Bell Towers and Prince Gong's Residence. Qianhai Lake is where locals go for a dip in the summer or for a drink in the cafés that line its shores. The ultra-modern Wangfujing Dajie slices through the east of this district, with its fashionable shops and hotels.

To the east, **Chaoyang** caters to Beijing's foreign residents, with the Russian quarter still clinging to the north side of Ritan Park. Chaoyang is where you more often come to shop and dine than to sightsee. The notable exception is Dongyue Temple, smack in the middle of the district. Within this area and to the northeast of the Workers' Stadium, **Sanlitun Embassy Area** is crowded with trendy bars and restaurants, while **Jianguomenwai Embassy Area** to the south is lined with prominent shops and malls.

To the southeast of the Forbidden City, **Chongwen** is quickly coming under the wrath of bulldozers, with new apartment complexes replacing older courtyard houses. The main draws to this area are the Temple of Heaven and Panjiayuan Market. West of here, **Xuanwu** includes the chaotic **Qianmen** neighbourhoods of Dazhalan Market and Liulichang, with Niujie Mosque in the south and the China Millennium Monument in the north. To the northwest of the Forbidden City is the suburban **Haidian District**, home to the zoo, aquarium and university, and stretching all the way to the Summer Palace and Fragrant Hills Park.

Beaten Track

Looking to get away from the hyper, baseball-capped tourist groups and postcard-pushing vendors? Finding a solitary getaway isn't an easy feat in Beijing, but you can find quieter, locals-only crevices. Relax on a bench in Ritan or Zhongshan Park during the day or hire a paddleboat and float peacefully around the Yuyuan Lake. Linger endlessly over a cup of aromatic tea in the soothing Green Tea House or mull over the artwork in the calming Red Gate Gallery.

Taking a break on the tourist trail

Hutongs

Squeezed between wide boulevards, high-rises and shopping centres lies the labyrinth of Beijing's vibrant *hutongs* (alleyways). Each one is home to a mini-community with an ancient and often colourful past. The word *hutong* was likely brought to Beijing from Mongolia, where it refers to water wells and, by extension, the small villages surrounding them. Chinese characters for the word *hutong* weren't adopted until the 1930s, when the Western practice of posting street names began.

Hutongs were generally given utilitarian names such as Cujiang (Vinegar Shop), Jianchang (Arrow Factory) and Zaoshu (Date Tree), offering not-too-subtle hints as to the landmarks or trades you could find along them. Other *hutongs* were named after their shape or size, such as Koudai (Pocket), referring to a dead-end *hutong*, or Biandan (Bamboo Pole), referring to a long, narrow *hutong*. The resulting difficulty was (and is) distinguishing between the many *hutongs* with identical names – for example, there are 11 *hutongs* named Biandan.

During the Cultural Revolution, many communities changed the names of their *hutongs* to something with a more revolutionary ring to it, such as Miezi Hutong (Destroy the Capitalist Lane) or Hongxiaobing Hutong (Little Red Guard Lane).

Hutongs are traditionally lined with *siheyuan* (four-sided courtyard homes). Originally, the height of the *siheyuan* walls, the size of the door and the shape of the door stones all told of the type of merchant, official or family that lived inside. Until recently, a *siheyuan* could only be one storey; anything greater was considered presumptuous, as inhabitants would be able to look down on the emperor, should he happen by. Other rules have also relaxed over time, such as the required *hutong* width (some have measured in at just 50cm wide) and direction (they once all ran east–west in accordance with feng shui).

As department stores and faceless high-rises clamour into town behind bulldozers and wrecking crews, it's difficult not to sigh with regret at the steady disappearance of Beijing's *hutongs*. Families rooted here for countless generations are being packed up and moved to apartment compounds far from the centre. And yet, while we lament the loss of the unique charm of these old quarters, these families may welcome the chance to escape the dangerous coal heating, inadequate or non-existent plumbing, and precarious wiring that remain prevalent in many *hutongs*.

Despite this woeful situation, there are still some *hutongs* for you to wander around (see p34); in fact, if anything is going to save *hutongs* from oblivion, it's the keen interest tourists have taken in them. On warm evenings, when families escape the heat of their *siheyuan* and take to the *hutong*, rent a bike and explore old Beijing.

Bicycle and cart riders making their way down Xiaojiao Hutong

MUSEUMS

Ancient Coin Museum
(4, A4) From early shellfish coins to silver and gold, the museum houses over 10,000 coins from the past 3000 years. Upstairs are views across the city and a small historical exhibition on Beijing's architecture, as well as the Beijing East Gallery (p28). Outside you can browse through the ancient-coin market.
✉ **Deshengmen Jianlou**
☎ 6201 8073
Ⓜ Jishuitan ◷ Tues-Sun 9am-4pm $ Y10

Ancient Observatory
(4, H12) The observatory was built in 1437 to facilitate both astrological predictions and seafaring navigation. The Chinese explored the skies with cutting-edge instruments and empirical rigorousness, and many Ming and Qing emperors relied heavily on the predictions of astrologers to plan their military moves. Climb up to the roof for impressive astronomical instruments set against a backdrop of the modern cityscape.
✉ **Jianguomen Beidajie, near Jianguomen Nei Dajie**
☎ 6512 6923
Ⓜ Jianguomen ◷ Apr-Sept 9am-6pm, Oct-Mar 9-11am & 1-4pm $ Y10/5; preschool children free

Beijing Songtangzhai Museum (4, K5)
This small museum of folk carving draws together over 1000 wood and stone pieces from across China. On display are doorways, screens, panels and objects whose carvings embody traditional legends and images. Some of the pieces are over 2000 years old.
✉ **14 Liulichang Dongjie** ☎ 8316 4663
Ⓜ Hepingmen ◷ 9.30am-5pm $ Y10

Confucius say...

Chinese Revolution & History Museum (4, H7)
Under renovation at the time of research, temporary exhibitions here include displays on Inner Mongolia and the Tang dynasty. The museum is scheduled to reopen sometime in 2003.
✉ **Tiananmen Square (east side)** ☎ 6512 8321
Ⓜ Tiananmen Dong ◷ Tues-Sun 8.30am-4.30pm $ Y10-20

Imperial Archives
(4, H8) This well-preserved courtyard building is the former repository for imperial records, decrees and encyclopaedic works. The Jade Book records the imperial family tree – not the easiest task considering the level of extra-marital activity within the Forbidden City. The book weighs 150kg and is 1m thick.
✉ **136 Nanchizi Dajie**
Ⓜ Tiananmen Dong ◷ 9am-7pm $ free

Imperial College (4, A9)
Built by the grandson of Kublai Khan in 1306, this is where the emperor annually expounded the Confucian classics to an audience of thousands of kneeling students, professors and court officials.
✉ **Guozijian Jie**
Ⓜ Yonghegong ◷ 9am-5.30pm $ Y6

The stately Imperial College

Lu Xun Museum (4, E1)
Lu Xun (1881-1936) is often regarded as the father of modern Chinese literature. Having aligned himself with the Communist cause, he is chiefly remembered for *The True Story of Ah Q*. Unfortunately, the museum is hampered by its shortage of English captions.
✉ 19 Gongmenkou Eriao
☎ 6616 4168 Ⓜ Fu-chengmen ◷ Tues-Sun 9am-4pm 💲 Y5

Military Museum (3, G6)
Missiles, tanks and fighter planes are eyed up by statues of Mao and his buddies on the ground floor of this museum. Upstairs, the halls glorify conflicts such as the Opium War and the war against US involvement in Korea. English captions are limited.

The long and tall of the Military Museum

Peking Man
In the 1920s and 1930s, Chinese archaeologists unearthed skulls, stone tools and animal bones believed to be between 500,000 and 230,000 years old. Was this the birthplace of civilisation? Unfortunately, we're unlikely to ever know. Research was never carried out on Peking Man's skull because, on the eve of the Japanese invasion, the remains mysteriously disappeared – some fear to the bottom of the sea, with Americans on the run. Protected by Unesco, the caves and museum halls at Zhoukoudian, where the remains were discovered, are open to visitors. Zhoukoudian is 48km southwest of Beijing (1, E2; 🚌 917 from Tianqiao station to Fangshan, then taxi 6km; ◷ 8.30am-4.30pm; 💲 Y20).

✉ 9 Fuxing Lu
☎ 6851 4441
Ⓜ Junshibowuguan
◷ 8.30am-5pm 💲 Y5

National Aviation Museum (1, C2)
Deep in a hangar carved into a mountainside and on the runways of a 'secret' fighter airstrip are over 300 old warplanes that kids and enthusiastic adults can climb on. This raved-about museum is located a distant 60km north of downtown.
✉ Xiaotangshan, Changping District
☎ 6178 1054 🚌 345 from Deshengmen station, then bus 912
◷ 8am-5.30pm
💲 Y40/20

Natural History Museum (6, C2) This huge building is filled with fossils, stuffed animals and computer-animated dinosaurs that kids will love. For those with a strong (and preferably empty) stomach, head over to the human anatomy display, where you can see human cadavers and spliced genitalia. There are limited English captions but you can probably guess what you're looking at.
✉ 126 Tianqiao Nandajie ☎ 6702 3096
Ⓜ Qianmen, then bus 20 ◷ 8.30am-5pm
💲 Y15/10 adults/seniors & children under 1.2m

Wangfujing Palaeolithic Museum (4, H9)
This archaeological site displays artefacts, bone tools and fossils discovered in 1996 during the construction of the Oriental Plaza. There are also skull casts of Peking Man and two frighteningly well-preserved 200-year-old bodies from a site in eastern Beijing. There are no English translations.
✉ Basement, Oriental Plaza, 1 Dongchang'an Jie
☎ 8518 6306 Ⓜ Wangfujing, northeast exit
◷ Mon-Fri 10am-4.30pm, Sat-Sun 10am-6.30pm 💲 Y10 ♿ good

GALLERIES

Art Gallery of the China Millennium Monument

(3, G6) In addition to a permanent collection of Oriental and Occidental art, the Gallery of Modern Art and the Multi-Media Digital Art Gallery host touring exhibitions from around the globe.

✉ 9a Fuxing Jie
☎ 6851 3322
🖥 www.bj2000.org.cn
Ⓜ Junshibowuguan
🕑 8am-6pm 💲 Y50

Beijing East Gallery

(4, A4) A dimly lit but interesting collection of modern Chinese paintings, set in the atmospheric north watchtower.

✉ Deshengmen Jianlou, Bei'erhuan Zhonglu ☎ 6201 4962 Ⓜ Jishuitan 🕑 Tues-Sun 9am-6pm 💲 free

China Art Gallery

(4, E8) Under renovation at the time of writing, this collection of paintings is often raved about and should be reopened by the time you read this.

✉ 1 Wusi Dajie
☎ 6401 7076 🚌 103, 104, 106, 108 🕑 Tues-Sun 9am-5pm

Courtyard Gallery (7, E6)

Avant-garde exhibitions nestled next to the Forbidden City moat.

✉ 95 Donghuamen Dajie ☎ 6526 8882 Ⓜ Tiananmen Dong, then bus 60 🕑 Mon-Sat 11am-7pm, Sun noon-7pm 💲 free

Creation Gallery (4, F13)

Opened and curated by the son of celebrated artist Li Keran, this gallery exhibits and sells paintings fresh off the easel. This is a good place to see what local painters are up to.

✉ Ritan Donglu
☎ 6506 7570
🖥 kecg_cn@sina.com
Ⓜ Jianguomen, then bus 29 🕑 10am-7pm
💲 free 🦽 good

Kuaixue Hall (4, D5)

Wang Da Guan (1925-97) excelled at figure painting. His paintings reflect everyday life in Beijing in the early 20th century. Amazingly detailed, one painting measures a full 14m long. Prints are for sale.

✉ Beihai Park (north gate) 🚌 118 🕑 9am-4.45pm 💲 free

Wan Fung Art Gallery

(4, H8) Set in an imperial courtyard of the Imperial Archives, this gallery exhibits contemporary art.

✉ 136 Nanchizi Dajie
☎ 6523 3320 🖥 www .wanfung.com.cn
Ⓜ Tiananmen Dong
🕑 9am-5pm 💲 free

Wenchang Gallery (5, C4)

A tranquil annex to the Summer Palace, this gallery is modelled after a Qing courtyard. Inside is a beautiful collection of artefacts, including carvings, bronze and iron pieces, intricate screens and pottery. Many of the items on display were looted during the Opium War and only recently returned from private European collections.

✉ Kunming Lu, next to Summer Palace east entrance ☎ 6288 1144 ext 224 Ⓜ Xizhimen, then bus 375 🕑 8.30am-4.30pm 💲 Y20

Xu Beihong Museum

(4, B3) Best remembered for his galloping horses, Xu Beihong (1895-1953) injected dynamism into Chinese painting. He's celebrated here in seven halls that display oils, gouache, pen and ink sketches and portraits.

✉ 53 Xinjiekou Beidajie
☎ 6225 2265 Ⓜ Jishuitan 🕑 Tues-Sun 9am-noon & 1-5pm 💲 Y5

Photographic exhibition at the Courtyard Gallery

HISTORICAL BUILDINGS & MONUMENTS

Beijing Exhibition Hall
(3, E7) This building is noticeable from way down the block for its unlikely Russian exterior.
✉ Xizhimen Wai Dajie
Ⓜ Xizhimen

Bell Tower (4, B6)
Built in the late 1200s, the Bell Tower was razed and rebuilt in the 18th century. Built along the north–south axis of the imperial buildings, this bell once tolled on ceremonial occasions.
✉ Gulou Dongdajie
☎ 6401 2674
Ⓜ Andingmen, then bus 58; or Tiananmen Xi, then bus 5 ⏱ 9am-4.30pm $ Y6; incl Drum Tower Y10

China Millennium Monument (3, G6)
This gargantuan sundial is one of Beijing's most impressive modern structures. It supposedly turns once every 2.655 hours. Inside, beneath a lit model of the night sky, is a fantastic carved mural of 40 celebrated figures from China's cultural history. From the top of the dial are some great views across Beijing.
✉ 9a Fuxing Jie
☎ 6851 3322 🖳 www .bj2000.org.cn Ⓜ Junshi-bowuguan ⏱ 7am-6pm
$ Y30/20; children under 1.2m Y15

**Dongbianmen
(Southeast Watchtower)**
(4, J12) This Ming-dynasty watchtower is punctured with 144 archer's windows

The splendidly restored Drum Tower

and was once a part of the city wall. You can hunt down 'I was here' graffiti left by the international troops of the Allied Forces that overwhelmed the tower during the Boxer Rebellion. The impressive interior is home to a slightly less-impressive exhibition of the area's history. When you buy your ticket at the bottom of the stairs, you may need to ask staff to switch on the lights. Note that captions are in Chinese only.
✉ 3rd fl, Dongbianmen, Jianguomen Beidajie
☎ 8512 1554 Ⓜ Bei-jingzhan ⏱ Tues-Sun 9am-5pm $ Y5/2

Drum Tower (4, B6)
Originally built in 1273 to mark the centre of the Mongol capital of Dadu, the tower has since been repeat-edly destroyed and restored. The drums were once

beaten to mark the hours of the day; today, only one drum remains. Stagger up the steep steps for long views over Beijing's rooftops.
✉ Gulou Dongdajie
☎ 6401 2674
Ⓜ Andingmen, then bus 58; or Tiananmen Xi, then bus 5 ⏱ 9am-4.30pm $ Y6; incl Bell Tower Y10

Great Hall of the People
(4, H6) Home of the National People's Congress, this fairly mundane building is open to the public when the Congress is not sitting. Many of the halls are named after Chinese provinces and regions and are decorated appropriately.
✉ Tiananmen Square (western side) ☎ 6309 6668 Ⓜ Tiananmen Xi ⏱ 8am-3pm $ Y30/15; compulsory bag check Y2-5

Bare-Foot Belle
According to the legend of the Bell Tower, as the bell-maker cast the 42-ton bell, his daughter plunged head first into the molten iron. He made a grab for her but only managed to hang onto her shoe as she slid into the furnace. Since then, the soft chime of the Ming-dynasty bell is said to sound like *xie*, the Chinese word for shoe.

Party On!

You may wonder what that giant chunk of greenery is to the west of the Forbidden City. If you wander over, you'll be allowed to gawk at the entrance, framed by the **Tower of the Treasured Moon Gate** (1758), but the armed People's Liberation Army soldiers won't let you go any further. Instead, they'll tell you these are the Party Grounds. Please note that this isn't an invitation to boogie down. This Party is exclusive and these grounds have been nicknamed the New Forbidden City, where only the highest Communist Party Officials reside and have offices. Not exactly the kind of party you want to crash.

Monument to the People's Heroes (4, H7)

In the centre of Tiananmen Square, this monument stands on the site of the original Outer Palace Gate. Built in 1958, its 36m granite obelisk is carved with scenes of key revolutionary events such as the Chinese destroying opium in the 19th century.

✉ Tiananmen Square
Ⓜ Tiananmen Dong
♿ excellent

Qianmen (Front Gate) (4, J7)

Built in the 15th century, this gate once divided the ancient Inner City and the outer suburban zone. The city walls have long since disappeared, however the majestic and unyielding Qianmen has become a compass point in Beijing. Made up of two structures, Arrow Tower to the south and Zhengyang Gate to the north, they're impressive to walk through.

✉ Qianmen ☎ 6525 3176 Ⓜ Qianmen
🕑 8am-4pm 💲 free to walk through; Zhengyang Gate Y5

Silver Ingot Bridge

(4, B6) Dividing Qianhai and Houhai Lakes is this picturesque, white marble bridge. It has suffered a pounding from feet and carts over the past couple of centuries and was last rebuilt in 1984.

✉ Houhai & Qianhai Lakes 🚌 5, 118 ♿ good

Zhengyi Ci Theatre (4, K5)

Ornate and colourful, this opera house, originally a Ming temple, was reconstructed as a theatre during the Qing dynasty. You can have a look inside during the day but it's best viewed during an opera (p91).

✉ 220 Qianmen Xiheyan Jie ☎ 8315 3150 🖥 beijingopera _zytt@yahoo.com.cn
Ⓜ Hepingmen 🕑 10am-4pm 💲 Y10

PLACES OF WORSHIP

Confucius Temple

(4, A9) Following Qufu (the birthplace of the master), this is the second-largest Confucian temple in China. With ancient cypresses and a Forest of Steles (stretching 630,000 characters across 189 2.4m tablets), it's also a peaceful, if somewhat forlorn, sanctuary. Sadly, the steles outside are being washed clean by acid rain and about a quarter of the carved characters have disappeared over the past decade.

✉ 13 Guozijian Jie
☎ 8401 1977
Ⓜ Yonghegong
🕑 8.30am-5pm
💲 Y10/3

Dazhong Temple (Great Bell Temple) (3, C7)

Weighing in at 46.5 tons, come and check out China's biggest bell yet. It's so big that when it was cast in 1406 a special canal had to be built and allowed to freeze in order to transport the bell by sled from the foundry to this temple. The bell is decorated with Buddhist sutras and Sanskrit incantations. Also on view is a collection of Marquis Zeng of Yi's bells and a small exhibition on bell casting (Y2).

✉ 31a Beisanhuan Xilu
☎ 6255 0819 🚌 302, 300, 367 🕑 8.30am-4.30pm 💲 Y10

Dongjiaomin Catholic Church (St Michael's)
(4, J9) There are daily masses held at this twin-spired, peaceful church. It's not much of a sight, but a pleasant place for worshippers to come together.
✉ Dongjiaomin Xiang
Ⓜ Dongdan, then bus 9, 103 or 104 ☯ Chinese Mass Mon-Sat 6.30am, Sun 8am & 6pm; Latin Mass Sat & Sun 7am; Korean Mass Sun 10.30am; Eucharist Sun 7.50am, Thurs 8-9am
💲 free

Fayuan Temple (3, H9)
Still a hive of activity, this temple was built in the 7th century and is now home to the China Buddhism College. Student monks in yellow robes play table tennis and gossip in the courtyards. In the back hall is an unusual copper Buddha seated on a delicate 1000-petal lotus flower.
✉ 7 Fayuansi Qianjie
☎ 6353 3966
Ⓜ Changchunjie, then bus 61 ☯ Thurs-Tues 8.30-11.30am & 1.30-3.30pm 💲 Y5

Guangji Temple (4, E3)
The current headquarters of the Chinese Buddhist Association, this simple temple has a history of over 800 years, and a shaded courtyard to linger in.
✉ Fuchengmen Nei Dajie ☎ 6616 0907
Ⓜ Fuchengmen, then bus 102 or 103
☯ 8.30am-4.30pm
💲 free

Niujie Mosque (3, H8)
An ornate, fascinating blend of Muslim and Chinese styles, with flourishes of Arabic and a profusion of greenery, this mosque dates back to the 10th century. The largest of about 40 mosques around town, it's here, in the Building for Observing the Moon, that the lunar calendar was calculated. Dress appropriately (no shorts or short skirts) or borrow the trousers loaned out at the gate. The main prayer hall is open to Muslims only.
✉ 88 Niu Jie ☎ 6353 2564 Ⓜ Changchunjie, then bus 61 ☯ 8am-sunset 💲 Y10; free for Muslims

North Cathedral (4, E4)
Its grey flaking paint isn't exactly enticing, but this august cathedral is worth a look inside. Built in 1887, it suffered the brutalities of the Cultural Revolution and even had a stint as a factory warehouse – incredibly, some of the stained glass has survived. Latin and Chinese masses

St Joseph's Church

are held each morning.
✉ Xishiku Dajie
Ⓜ Fuchengmen, then bus 103; or Xidan, then bus 47 💲 free

St Joseph's Church (4, F9)
Having been burned and demolished umpteen times, the East Cathedral is fully repaired and open for business. The front courtyard is a favourite hangout for teenage skateboarders and exhausted shoppers.
✉ 74 Wangfujing Dajie
Ⓜ Wangfujing
☯ Mon-Sat 6.30-7am, Sun 6.30-8am 💲 free

The Hui of Beijing

The largest of 10 Muslim minority groups in China, you are likely to encounter Hui vendors on the streets of Beijing selling delicious nougat and roasted nuts. With Muslims numbering between 15 million (officially) and 35 million (unofficially) across China, there are an estimated 180,000 Hui in Beijing alone. As ethnic-Chinese, the Hui differ from other Muslim groups in China and are easily distinguishable by their white caps. If you'd like to impress the Hui at Niujie Mosque, greet them with *salaam aleikum* (may peace be upon you).

Pot Luck

If all the luck has rubbed off your rabbit's foot, keep your eyes open around Beijing's temples for opportunities to bolster your good fortune. At Azure Clouds Temple (p22) you can liberate a goldfish from a tank into the pond; on Jade Islet (p18) you can rub a smiling buddha's belly; in Taoist temples, such as White Cloud Temple (p21), hit the hanging bell with a coin; or touch the Tree of Prosperity at Tanzhe Temple (p50). The trickiest, luck-laden task to master is outside Kuaixue Hall in Beihai Park (4, D5), where you can try to make water boil and sing by rubbing your damp palms around the rim of a bronze pot.

South Cathedral (4, J3)
Matteo Ricci was the Jesuit missionary who introduced Christianity to China. The church built on the site of his abode has been burned to the ground three times. It has once again been reconstructed and offers a welcome place of prayer for Christians. Enter by the side door.
✉ 141 Qianmen Xidajie

Ⓜ Xuanwumen
☯ Latin Mass Mon-Fri mornings, Sun 6am; English Mass Sun 10am
$ free

Wanshou Temple (3, E6)
Originally consecrated for the storage of Buddhist texts, this is where the imperial gang would take a tea break en route to the Summer Palace. The reason to visit is to see the prized collection of bronze Buddhist statuary, including some rather exotic Tantric pieces.
✉ Xisanhuan Beilu
☎ 6841 3380
Ⓜ Gongzhufen, then bus 944 ☯ Tues-Sun 9am-4.30pm $ Y10

Wen Tianxiang Temple
(4, C8) This tiny, serene family shrine is dedicated to Southern song poet Wen Tianxiang (1236-83), who was captured by the Mongols and incarcerated in Beijing. In the grounds stands an ancient jujube tree, supposedly cultivated by Wen himself. All inscriptions and explanations are in Chinese.
✉ 63 Fuxue Hutong
☎ 6401 4968
Ⓜ Andingmen, then bus 108; or Dongdan, then bus 101 ☯ Tues-Sun 9am-5pm $ Y1

PARKS & PUBLIC SPACES

Ditan Park (Temple of Earth) (3, D11)
At the opposite end of the cosmos and the compass to the Temple of Heaven, Ditan Park is the site of imperial sacrifices to the Earth God. It's not as spectacular as its southerly sister, except during the Chinese New Year temple fair and the sparkling Ice Festival in winter.
✉ Andingmen Wai Dajie ☎ 6421 4657
Ⓜ Yonghegong
☯ 9am-9pm $ Y1
♿ good

Grand View Garden
(3, J8) New on the scene, this park opened in 1988 and is designed to look like the family gardens in the classic Chinese novel *Dream of the Red Mansion* by Cao Zueqin. It's a lovely place to relax.
✉ 12 Nancaiyuan Jie
☎ 6354 4994 🚌 59 from Qianmen
☯ 8.30am-4.30pm
$ Y10 ♿ good

Jingshan Park (4, E6)
Offering a gorgeous view over the golden rooftops of

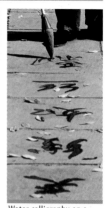
Water calligraphy on a Jingshan Park pathway

the Forbidden City and beyond, the hill in the centre of this park was created from the earth excavated to construct the palace moat. The hill protects the palace from the evil spirits (and dust storms) of the north. This beautiful and calm park is a great place to see Beijing's elderly exercising and stretching their legs up around their ears. In the east of the park is a locust tree where the last Ming emperor hanged himself as rebels swarmed at the city walls.

✉ Jingshan Xijie
☎ 6403 3225
Ⓜ Tiananmen Xi, then bus 5 ⏱ 6am-10pm
$ Y2 ♿ around the park but not up the hill

Longtan Park (3, J12)
Popular with local families, this well-kept park is a lovely place to rent a paddleboat or wander around. There's a kiddie's playground (8am-8pm; Y5) near the western entrance. In autumn there's an explosion of lotuses in the southeastern pond.

✉ Longtan Lu
Ⓜ Beijingzhan, then bus 63 ⏱ 6am-10pm
$ Y2 ♿ good

Old Summer Palace
(3, A5) In the 18th century Emperor Qianlong decided it might be nice to have a European palace, so he asked some Jesuits to design one for him. They went all out with elaborate fountains and baroque statuary. Unfortunately, during the Second Opium

---

> ### High-story
> The world's first spacecraft continue to hover above Beijing's parks, resembling birds, butterflies and explosions of colour. Invented by the Chinese during the Han dynasty, it took some time to discover what the kite was. It was first tried as a surveying tool and a messenger, but, controlled more by the wind than the flyer, this was fairly unsuccessful. Next, someone strapped a kite to his back and jumped off a cliff in an attempt to fly; this was even more unsuccessful. It wasn't until the Tang dynasty, over 700 years later, that the kite was finally recognised as a toy.

War it was pummelled to bits. All that remains is a melancholic array of broken columns and marble chunks. The best-preserved relic is the Great Fountain Ruins and also worth checking out is the nearby reproduction of the 10,000 Flowers Maze.

✉ Yiheyuan Lu
☎ 6262 8501
Ⓜ Xizhimen, then minibus 375 🚌 4 from Qianmen ⏱ 7am-7pm
$ park Y10; palace ruins Y15 ♿ park good; ruins OK

Ritan Park (4, F13)
Built in 1530 as an altar for ritual sacrifice to the sun, this lovely, pine-filled park is a peaceful diversion. The altar is usually surrounded by kite-flyers and a gaggle of laughing children.

✉ Ritan Lu Ⓜ Jianguomen, then bus 29
⏱ 6am-9pm $ Y1
♿ good

Tiananmen Square
(4, H7) Kites flit through the sky, children stamp around on the pavement and tourists snap photos in the world's largest public square. It's a desert out there, conceived by Mao to project the enormity of the Communist Party. During the Cultural Revolution, Mao reviewed parades of up to a million young Red Guards here. In 1976 another million people came here to pay their last respects to Mao. In 1989 army tanks and soldiers cut down pro-democracy demonstrators, leaving the world with no doubt that the Communist Party had every intention of staying in power despite market reforms. You'll get to know Tiananmen Square well as you traverse back and forth to the many sights surrounding it.

✉ Tiananmen
Ⓜ Tiananmen Xi, Tiananmen Dong
$ free ♿ excellent

Workers' Cultural Palace
(4, G7) Ignore the uninviting name and come to this restful park for a quiet

escape. Once the emperors' premier place of worship, the hall of the Supreme Temple remains, although it's only open to the public when there's an exhibition.

- ✉ Dongchang'an Jie
- ☎ 6512 4970
- Ⓜ Tiananmen Dong
- ◔ 6.30am-7.30pm
- 💲 Y2

Yuyuantan Park (3, F6)
Shady trees, benches, wide paths and big lakes make this a very pretty park to get lost in. You can rent paddleboats, pedal- or battery-powered boats (Y10/20/30) or take a cruise on the lakes (Y5). There's also a fantastic outdoor water park with slides and pools (June-Jul 9am-8pm, Aug-Sept 9am-10pm; Y15/10 adults/children under 1.4m).

- ✉ Xisanhuan Zhonglu
- Ⓜ Junshibowuguan
- ◔ 6am-10pm 💲 Y2/1; children under 1.2m free
- ♿ good

Zhongshan Park (4, G6)
Hedging up against the moat of the Forbidden City, this is a small oasis away from the crowds. An emperor once offered sacrifices to the God of Land and the God of Five Grains here; the ruins of the altar remain and workmen are busy restoring the temple.

- ✉ Xichang'an Jie
- ☎ 6512 4970 Ⓜ Tiananmen Xi ◔ 6am-10pm
- 💲 Y3; incl private gardens Y5 ♿ OK

Zizhuyuan Park (3, E6)
Next door to the zoo, this is a fairly well-kept, spacious getaway, complete with lotuses and bamboo. Plunk yourself down beside one of the three lakes or waterways and join the locals in fishing, reading or simply relaxing.

- ✉ Zizhuyuan Lu
- Ⓜ Xizhimen, then any trolleybus west ◔ 6am-10pm 💲 Y2 ♿ OK

Serenity in Zhongshan

HUTONGS

According to an old Beijing saying, there are 360 famous *hutongs* in the city and as many nameless *hutongs* as hairs on a cow. Well, the cow appears to have creeping alopecia as the *hutongs* steadily disappear, replaced with boulevards and apartment blocks. See them while you can. For more on *hutongs*, see p25.

Dajingchang Hutong (4, B7) Named after a printing factory that produced Buddhist scriptures, this narrow and twisting *hutong* gives you a glimpse at some open courtyard gardens.

- ✉ north off Gulou Dongdajie Ⓜ Andingmen, then bus 123 ♿ good

Dongjixiang Hutong (4, D7) Once the home of imperial eunuchs, this leafy residential *hutong* is quiet and well cared for. Just south of here is Dong-banqiao Xixian, where prospective servant girls to the emperor were sent from around the country.

- ✉ south of (parallel to) Di'anmen Dongdajie
- 🚌 5, 118 ♿ good

Dongsi Batiao (4, D10) Dating back to the Ming dynasty, this *hutong* was once home to Mei Lanfang, a Beijing opera star, and later held the offices of Tian Han, composer of China's national anthem. Today it's lively and busy with chickens and mah jong players.

- ✉ south of (parallel to) Dongsishitiao Lu 🚌 113, 115, 118 ♿ good

Fuxue Hutong (4, C9) Running past Wen Tianxiang Temple, this *hutong* has some great tiled rooftops.

- ✉ east off Jiaodaokou Nandajie Ⓜ Andingmen, then bus 108 ♿ good

Ju'er Hutong (4, B8)

Numbers 3, 6 and 7 along this carefully preserved *hutong* were once the mansions of a Zhili Governor. Today you can see many two-storey courtyard homes here.

✉ btw Nanluogu Xiang & Jiaodaokou Nandajie Ⓜ Andingmen, then bus 108 ♿ good

Liuyin Jie (4, B5)

This wide, willow-lined *hutong* runs quietly past Prince Gong's residence.

✉ btw Yangfang Hutong & Dingfu Jie Ⓜ Gulou Dajie, then bus 58 🚌 13, 118 ♿ good

Mao'er Hutong (4, C7)

The elaborate doors along this *hutong* make it quite obvious that it has always been the dwelling place of the well-off. Even the neighbourhood toilets look posh! Have a look at No 5, a well-preserved courtyard home dating back to the Qing dynasty. No 13 was the home of Feng Guozhang, a Northern Warlord. Empress Wan Rong, the last emperor's wife, was born and raised along here. At the eastern end, Nanluogu Xiang is a lively *hutong*.

✉ west off Nanluogu Xiang Ⓜ Andingmen, then bus 108 ♿ good

Qianliang Hutong

(4, D9) This is where *qianliang* (coins) were stored during the Ming dynasty. There are still many old, tile-roofed

Choosing Ms Right

Concubines, or 'palace maids', were generally between the ages of 13 and 16 when they first joined the ranks. Candidates were put through an elaborate selection process that ruled out girls considered too fat, too thin, too short or tall, those who spoke hoarsely or with the slightest stutter, those with large toes, thick wrists or stinky armpits. An average of 50 would be chosen from up to 5000 contenders. During the Tang dynasty, the imperial harem reached 40,000, while Qing Emperor Guongzu had only two concubines. Those concubines who fell into disfavour were often forced to live in distant palace buildings; thousands of others were beaten to death or died of starvation.

buildings along this wide *hutong*.

✉ btw Meishuguan Houjie & Dongsi Nandajie Ⓜ Dongdan, then bus 101 ♿ good

Wudaoying Hutong

(4, A9) *Wudaoying*, or Five Soldier's Way, refers to the five ways of martial arts. This residential *hutong* was the home of Ming dynasty martial-arts soldiers.

✉ south of Andingmen Dongdajie Ⓜ Yonghegong ♿ good

Xiaojiao Hutong (4, E8)

This leafy *hutong* is only about 100m long. As women with bound feet were once considered beautiful, Xiaojiao (little feet) refers to the young girls who lived here and were popular with the emperor. Just north, Dajiao (big feet) is where the less-popular girls lived.

✉ east off Donghuangchenggen Beijie 🚌 58, 108 ♿ good

Yuge Sixiang (4, A6)

Named after a temple that was located around here, this *hutong* is extremely narrow (keep your fingers crossed that you don't have to pass any cyclists as you head down it). Nearby and deep in the *hutongs*, Guowang Xixiang was once home to the Yellow Bannerman clan. Today it's home to caged birds and some serious mah jong players.

✉ east of Jiugulou Dajie Ⓜ Gulou Dajie ♿ OK

Mah jong players do battle down a hutong

FORMER RESIDENCES

Guo Moruo (4, C5)
A politically correct writer despite his elite roots, Guo Moruo (1892-1978) was awarded the Stalin Peace Prize in 1951 and survived the Cultural Revolution without a scratch. Guo's garden home contains his many books and manuscripts. Outside his home is a large Spirit Wall that was intended to keep out evil ghouls. (Chinese ghosts can only travel in straight lines.)
✉ 18 Qianhai Xijie
☎ 6612 5392 Ⓜ Gulou Dajie, then bus 58; or Tiananmen Xi, then bus 5 🚌 13, 118 ◷ Tues-Sun 9am-4pm 💲 Y6

Lao She (4, F8)
Author of *Rickshaw Boy* and *Tea House* and a lecturer at London's School of Oriental and African Studies, Lao She (1899-1966) was one of Beijing's most famous 20th-century writers. Severely persecuted during the Cultural Revolution, he committed suicide by drowning himself in a lake. On display are first editions, personal belongings and photos, including a disturbing shot of his humiliation at the hands of the Red Guards on the eve of his death.
✉ 19 Fengfu Hutong, off Dengshikou Xijie
Ⓜ Wangfujing, then bus 2, 52 or 210 ◷ Tues-Sun 9am-4pm 💲 Y5

Mei Lanfang (4, C4)
An immensely popular actor of female roles, Mei (1894-1961) popularised Beijing Opera in the West and is even said to have influenced a certain Mr Chaplin. Mei Lanfang's courtyard home is stuffed to the gills with costumes, furniture and old opera programs.
✉ 9 Huguosi Lu
☎ 6618 0351 🚌 55
◷ Tues-Sun 9am-4pm
💲 Y5

Song Qingling (4, A5)
Venerated by the Chinese as the wife of Sun Yatsen, Madam Song remained in Communist China while her wayward sister married Chiang Kai-shek and fled to Taiwan. Madam lived in this garden courtyard from 1963 until her death in 1981. On display are personal items, clothing, books and pictures.
✉ 46 Beiheyan Lu
Ⓜ Gulou Dajie, then bus 58 & 5 ◷ Tues-Sun 9am-4pm 💲 Y8

MARKETS

Dazhilan (4, K6)
Crammed full of silk outlets, tea shops, department stores, food, medicine and clothing specialists, this market is a happy kind of chaos. Many of Beijing's oldest shops can be found here. Have a look at Ruifuxiang (5 Dazhilan Jie), with its green archway and columns. The eastern end of Dazhilan is for pedestrians only. Head north up the narrow alleys off Dazhilan Jie for market-stall mania.
✉ off Qianmen Dajie
Ⓜ Qianmen 💲 free
♿ OK

Donghua Yeshi Night Market (4, G8)
This place is a zoo. Grasshoppers, kidneys, smelly tofu, mystery meat on kebabs, yak butter and cheese — you may not want to buy lunch here but you'll definitely get an eyeful.
✉ Donganmen Dajie
Ⓜ Wang-fujing, then bus 101 ◷ 5.30-10.30pm
💲 free ♿ OK

Serving it all up at Donghua Yeshi Night Market

Hubble Bubble, Tummy Trouble?

Behind the doors of 24 Dazhilan Jie, an elderly man is mixing ancient and secret concoctions. While his list of ingredients reads like a witch's brew, the resulting potions won't expel evil spirits or turn his neighbour into a toad. Instead, they're tried and tested remedies for headaches, fear and pneumonia. Once the favoured chemist of China's royalty, this famous herbal medicine shop, known as Tongrentang, has been peddling pills since 1669. Feeling a bit queasy? Head here for an on-the-spot consultation.

Panjiayuan Market (3, J13)

The 'Dirt' Market is a fantastic place to browse through Beijing's past, from antique furniture to Cultural Revolution memorabilia. Amongst its 50,000 daily visitors are some of China's best barterers, whose tactics can be a sight in themselves.
✉ Panjiayuan Lu
Ⓜ Guo Mao, then bus 28 🕐 Sat-Sun dawn-3pm 💲 free ♿ OK

Yuting Huaniao Shichang (Flower & Bird Market)

(6, E4) This is where elderly men come to buy their songbirds. With turtles, rabbits, birds, garden decor and a vibrant array of flowers, it's a lovely place to explore.
✉ Yongdingmen Dongbinhe Lu Ⓜ Chongwenmen, then bus 39
🕐 7am-dusk 💲 free
♿ OK

Yuting Huaniao Shichang

QUIRKY BEIJING

Mao Zedong Mausoleum

(4, J6) This historical giant has been kept pickled and on display since his death in 1976. Join the queues of respectful Chinese mourners for a quick glimpse.
✉ Tiananmen Square

Hop aboard a pedal boat for a quacking good time!

☎ 6513 2277 Ⓜ Qianmen 🕐 Sept-June Tues-Sun 8.30-11.30am & 2-4pm; Jul-Aug Tues-Sun 8.30-11.30am 💲 free (must show passport); compulsory bag check Y10 ♿ good

Pedal Boats

(3, J9; 3, F6; 3, J12)
While most Westerners wouldn't consider a car to be a pretty pond ornament, they're all the rage in Beijing. In most parks around town you can pedal around the lake in one of these Flintstone-reminiscent vehicles. You can float in a giant duck, too.
✉ Taoranting Park, Yuyuantan Park, Longtan Park 🕐 9.30am-4.30pm

💲 Y10-40/hr, plus Y100-200 deposit

Underground City (4, J8)

In 1969 Mao decided that the future of Beijing lay underground. With a Soviet invasion looming and nuclear war on the mind, 2000 workers began burrowing an underground city by hand. A portion of this labyrinth is now open. Signposts to the Forbidden City and chambers labelled 'cinema' and 'hospital' give you an idea of the enormity of the project.
✉ btw 62 & 64 Xidamo-chang Jie, off Qianmen Dajie Ⓜ Qianmen 🕐 8am-5.30pm
💲 Y20/15

BEIJING FOR CHILDREN

Beijing Amusement Park (3, J12) This vintage park is next door to family-friendly Longtan Park. If your kids were bored with the Temple of Heaven, send them for a thrill on the looping roller coaster or enjoy the views from the Ferris wheel. If they can't get enough of it, head over to Chaoyang Amusement Park for more rides (3, E14; 8.30am-6pm).

✉ 1 Zuo'anmenwai Dajie ☎ 6711 1155 Ⓜ Chongwenmen, then bus 8 ☯ 8.30am-5.30pm $ Y60/40/free adults/children btw 1-1.4m & seniors/children under 1m

Beijing Aquarium (3, E7) Bypass the zoo and head next door to the largest inland aquarium in the world. There are piranhas in the Amazon rainforest, a shark aquarium, coral reefs and whales to keep your kids happy for hours.

✉ Xizhimenwai Dajie ☎ 6832 1960 Ⓜ Xizhimen, then any trolleybus west ☒ 4 from Qianmen ☯ Oct-May 9am-5.30pm, June-Sept 9am-6pm $ Y100/50

Beijing Sea View Water Park (1, C3) While you lounge on the beach, your little ones can entertain themselves with water-based jungle gyms, fishing pools, water slides and wave pools. If you're looking to get the whole family involved, there's tug-of-war and beach volleyball on weekends or you can rent an inflatable dinghy.

✉ 600 Lingyun, Capital Airport (6km north of Dashanzihuandao) ☎ 8431 9689 ☯ June-Aug 9am-8pm $ Y60/40/free adults/children/children under 1m

Blue Zoo Beijing (4, D13) If restaurant aquariums just aren't doing the trick, the sharks, eels and seahorses here should wake your kids up. The marine tunnel is Asia's longest and the twice-daily shark feedings are always a favourite.

✉ Workers' Stadium (south entrance), Gongren Tiyuchang ☎ 6591 3397 ext 1560 💻 www.blue-zoo.com Ⓜ Yong An Li, then bus 28 ☒ 118 ☯ 8am-8pm $ Y75/50/free adults/kids under 12 years/kids under 1m & seniors over 80 years

China Puppet Theatre (3, C10) This theatre regularly casts a spell over little (and not-so-little) ones. Call for a schedule.

✉ A1 Anhyui Xili ☎ 6425 3798 Ⓜ Gulou Dajie, then bus 380 or 406 ☯ evenings

Honey, I Brought the Kids

With neighbours and grandparents and aunts to mind the little ones, babysitting agencies are rare in Beijing. Nevertheless, you shouldn't have too much trouble finding a sitter. Most large hotels have English-speaking babysitters available for Y50/hr plus the sitter's cab ride home. Smaller hotels may not have an in-house service but should be able to offer you a personal recommendation. **Foreign Company Service** (☎ 6508 6664; Y15/hr) can also find you a sitter and, during the day, **Fundazzle** (p39) can assign a personal child minder if you book in advance.

ExploraScience
at Oriental Plaza

ExploraScience (4, H9)
Perfect for inquisitive kids, this Sony-sponsored, inter-active science exhibition is full of gadgets and activities.
✉ 1st fl, Oriental Plaza, 1 Dongchang'an Jie ☎ 8518 2255 🖳 www .explorascience.com 🅼 Wangfujing ⏲ Mon-Fri 9.30am-5.30pm, Sat-Sun 10am-7pm; closed 2nd Mon & Tues of every month 💲 Y30/20 ♿ good

Five Colour Earth Craft Centre (4, C12)
Pottery making, painting, and papermaking, run by a Chinese-Canadian couple. Most enjoyed by kids aged four and up.
✉ 1F, Bldg 10, Children's Palace, Dongzhimen Nandajie ☎ 6415 3839 🅼 Dongzhimen ⏲ 9am-6pm 💲 Y80/50 1/2hrs

Fundazzle (4, D14)
This indoor jungle gym will keep active tykes occupied on a rainy day. Kids need to bring socks but can leave their folks at home.
✉ Workers' Stadium (south entrance), Gongren Tiyuchang ☎ 6506 9066 🅼 Yong An Li, then bus 28

🚌 118 ⏲ Mon-Fri 9am-5.30pm, Sat-Sun & holidays 9am-7pm 💲 Y30/2hrs, babysitting Y20/hr (book in advance)

Gongti Yutai Bowling Centre (4, D13)
If chucking bowling balls down a lane gets your kids excited, bring them to this bright, new, 96-lane alley.
✉ 2nd fl, Workers' Stadium (west entrance), Gongren Tiyuchang Xilu ☎ 6552 1446 🅼 Yong An Li, then bus 118 ⏲ 8am-3am 💲 Y30; shoes Y5

Honey World (4, H9)
If your kids aren't as interested in shopping as you are, bring them here for arts and crafts, pottery, beadwork, interactive computer games, mini-bowling and a jungle gym. Activities are for kids aged three to 12 years.
✉ Basement, Oriental Plaza, 1 Dongchang'an Jie 🅼 Wangfujing ⏲ 9.30am-10pm 💲 Y10-30

Le Cool (4, H15)
Surrounded by shops that parents love, this popular ice rink is tops.
✉ Basement 2, China World Trade Centre, 1 Jianguomen Wai Dajie ☎ 6505 5776 🅼 Guo Mao ⏲ Mon, Wed, Fri & Sat 10am-10pm; Tues & Thurs 10am-5.50pm; Sun 10am-7.50pm 💲 Y30-50/90mins

Taoranting Park (3, J9)
You'll find a petting zoo (Y5) with carefree rabbits, monkeys and birds; jungle gyms with trampolines; pedal boats; a fantastic water park with pools and slides (9am-9pm; Y15) and lots of room to roam.
✉ Taiping Jie 🅼 Qianmen, then bus 59 ⏲ 6am-9pm 💲 Y2

Get skating at Le Cool

KEEPING FIT

Beijing Hikers
This organisation offers hikes in and around Beijing, including nearby villages. While the hikes are portrayed as 'easy', they'd give G.I. Jane a good workout. If you are up for it, pack plenty of water and join in some off-the-beaten-track adventures.
☎ 137 0100 3694
🖵 www.bjhikers.com

Beijing International Golf Club (1, C2)
Knock that little ball around this 18-hole, top-condition course. Surrounded by spectacular scenery, it is considered the best golfing Beijing has to offer.
✉ 35km north of Beijing, near Ming tombs
☎ 6067 2288 🚍 north to Changping, cross Seven Arch Bridge & turn east at North New Village towards Shisanling Reservoir Memorial
🕑 7am-2pm 💲 green fees Mon-Fri Y520, Sat-Sun & holidays Y800; clubs & shoes additional

Evolution Fitness Centre (3, G13)
Exercise on your own or join a class in aerobics, *ma dehong*, belly dancing, hip-hop dancing, t'ai chi, kick boxing, Latin dancing, yoga or aquaerobics. Personal training programs, fitness consultation and sports therapy are also available and there's a 25m, five-lane pool. This gym is raved about by lots of Westerners.
✉ Jianguomen Wai Dajie & Dongsanhuan Zhonglu ☎ 6567 0266/3499 🖵 www .evolution-fitness.com
Ⓜ Guo Mao 🕑 6.30am-10pm 💲 Y100/day

Fenxing Fencing Club (3, B10)
Interested in a bit of practise with your épée, sabre or foil stroke? This club offers equipment for those who know what to do with it and tuition for those who don't.
✉ 1 Anding Lu, Olympic Sports Centre ☎ 6491 2233 ext 480 Ⓜ Gulou Dajie, then bus 380

Pumping iron at Evolution Fitness Centre

Gongti Yutai Tennis Centre (4, D13)
Great location and really plush indoor court – too bad there's only one. Be sure to book ahead. Otherwise, try Chaoyang Tennis Club (1a Nongzhanguan Nanlu; 3, E14; ☎ 6501 0959) or the International Tennis Centre (50 Tiantan Lu; 6, C3; ☎ 6711 3872).
✉ 100 Gongren Tiyuchang Xilu (around the back) ☎ 6552 1446
Ⓜ Yong An Li, then bus 118 🕑 8am-10pm
💲 court Y260, tennis racket Y30

Nirvana Fitness & Spa (4, C15)
Hang out with Beijing's young professionals and watch DVDs or HBO while you take a walk on the treadmill. The equipment here is new, the sauna and steam rooms spotless and you'll be given a health test and workout schedule when you walk in the door. Aerobics, ballet, step, yoga, hip-hop, martial-arts and combat classes are regularly

From Mao suits to tracksuits

scheduled and hour-long massages can be booked.

✉ 2 Gongren Tiyuchang Beilu ☎ 6597 2008/2009 🖳 nirvana2001cn@yahoo.com.cn Ⓜ Dongsishitiao, then bus 118 🕑 8am-11pm $ Y100/day

Rent Bikes (4, B6)

Touring Beijing by bike can be side-splitting. Armed with a bell and a map, it's a fantastic way to tour *hutongs*, but do your best to avoid major thoroughfares. This place rents mountain bikes, tandem bikes, bikes with child seats and old clunkers. You can also rent bikes just north of Dazhalan Jie, on the west side of Qianmen Dajie (4, K6; ☎ 6218 5359; 7.30am-10pm).

✉ 6 Nanhouhai Hu ☎ 6613 7728 🚌 5, 118 🕑 9.30am-6pm $ Y30-50/day, plus Y150 deposit; tandem bikes Y30/hr

St Regis Health Spa & Club (4, H12)

After a match on the squash court, treat your muscles to a mud massage. You can also squash it up at the Pulse Club (Kempinski Hotel, 50 Liangmaqiao Lu;

Traditionally Healthy

You've just had your tongue examined and before that your pulse was taken 30 different ways. Now the doctor wants to consider your *yin* and your what? This is Traditional Chinese Medicine (TCM), scoffed at by many Western medics but tried and tested by millions of Chinese patients for thousands of years. Buying TCM off the shelf can be dangerous – while herbal medicine has relatively few side effects, there are often dos and don'ts attached to it. A safer option is to visit a TCM practitioner for a holistic remedy; just keep your fingers crossed that it's not snake gall-bladder tonic.

Clinics to try include **New World Eaton Medical Centre** (L5, Beijing New World Shopping Mall, 3 Chongwenmen Wai Jie; 4, K9; ☎ 6708 5075) or **Orient Traditional Chinese Medical Clinic** (Beijing Hotel, 33 Dongchang'an Jie; 4, H8; ☎ 6513 7766 ext 9119). You can also treat your feet to traditional therapy and massage at **Huaxialiangz** (A7 Gongti Xilu; 4, D13; ☎ 6552 5731).

3, D13; ☎ 6465 3888 ext 5722) or the Kerry Centre (1 Guanghua Lu; 4, G15; ☎ 6561 8833).

✉ St Regis Hotel, 21 Jianguomen Wai Dajie ☎ 6460 6688 Ⓜ Jianguomen $ squash Y160/45mins

Treasure Island Health Club (4, C12) Swim laps, work-out on the machines or unwind in the sauna.

✉ Asia Hotel, 8 Xinzhong Xijie, Gongti Beilu ☎ 6500 7788 🖳 www.bj-asiahotel .com.cn Ⓜ Dongsishitiao 🕑 gym & pool 6am-11pm; sauna 10am-2am $ gym & pool Y115/2hrs; sauna Y158/45mins ♿ OK

Yindong Indoor Swimming Pool

(3, B10) This Olympic-size pool has lots of lanes for lap swimmers and facilities for kids.

✉ 1 Anding Lu, Olympic Sports Centre ☎ 6495 5889/5890 Ⓜ Gulou Dajie, then bus 380 🕑 Mon-Fri 11am-11pm, Sat-Sun & holidays 10am-11pm $ Y30/20

Wheelin' and dealin' in the big city

Out & About

WALKING TOURS
'Mazing Hutongs

As long as you can negotiate one (very small) set of stairs, this tour is fantastic on a bike. Whether by foot or pedal, a compass will be handy in this labyrinth. Begin in the quietude of the Imperial College ❶ and Confucius Temple ❷. Head east, passing under the bright *pailou* (archway) at the end of Guozijian Jie. Follow the wafts of incense over the road to Lama Temple ❸. From here, head south and take a right down Fangjia Hutong. On the right, No 13 ❹ is a classic courtyard home. Cross over Andingmen Nei Dajie and continue west along Xiejia Hutong ❺. Take the next right and then the third left. Follow this with another right, and a quick left onto Guoxiang Hutong ❻, once a Mongolian emperor's address.

On watch at the Bell Tower

Turn left at the end and head south. At the T-junction take a right; this is Doufuchi Hutong ❼, home of Mao Zedong and his first wife. Take the first left south for the Bell Tower ❽ and Drum Tower ❾. Continue south and take the first right off Di'anmen Wai Dajie, up a short flight of stone stairs. Another right, followed by a left, will bring you to the Silver Ingot Bridge ❿. Cross over it and follow the path along the southwest shore of Qianhai Lake. Towards the end of it is La Rive Gauche ⓫ (p82), where some fine wine will help you unwind.

distance 4.5km **duration** 3½-4hrs
▶ start M Yonghegong
● end 🚌 118 from Di'anmen Xidajie; or 5 from Di'anmen Nei Dajie

Lakeside Amble

Head north past the knot of rickshaws and the Spirit Wall of Guo Moruo's former residence ❶. Turn left and follow the bend in this road north to the willow-lined Liuyin Jie ❷ and the gardens of Prince Gong's former residence ❸. Continue north, then follow Houhai Nanyan to Hou Hai Café & Bar ❹ (p81) for a drink. Cross over Silver Ingot Bridge ❺ and follow the southeast trail along Qianhai Lake, past the fishermen and mah jong battlers. At the southern end of the lake, head west to the pedestrian underpass, where you can cross Di'anmen Xidajie to Beihai Park ❻. The path heading southwest will bring you to the

SIGHTS & HIGHLIGHTS
Guo Moruo's former residence (p36)
Liuyin Jie (p35)
Prince Gong's former residence (p20)
Silver Ingot Bridge (p30)
Beihai Park (p18)

Wander over to Prince Gong's former residence

ferry dock, where you can hop on a boat to Jade Islet ❼. Dine at the imperial Fangshan Restaurant ❽ (p70) or at least poke your head in to gawk at the glittering gold decor. Climb up over the mountain, taking in the White Dagoba ❾, and across the bridge to Round City ❿, from where you can take a peek into the forbidden Zhongnanhai.

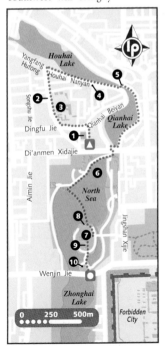

distance 3.8km **duration** 4hrs
▶ start 🚍 118 from Dongsishitiao; or 111 from Jishuitan
● end 🚇 5 to Tiananmen Xi

Tiananmen March

If you're planning on spending a few hours in the Forbidden City (very easily done), start this tour early in the day. That way, you'll wind up at Jingshan Park for sunset, when the views across the city are best. The march begins at Qianmen ❶, where you can pay your respects at Mao Zedong's Mausoleum ❷. Cross Tiananmen Square ❸, dodging kite strings and tour groups, for a gander at the Monument to the People's Heroes ❹. For those interested in socialist design, stop in at the Great Hall of the People ❺ before scaling Tiananmen ❻. Enter into the splendour of the Forbidden City ❼, take in the highlights and re-emerge at the western exit. Stop in for refreshments at the Purple Vine Teahouse ❽ (p83) before heading north to Jingshan Park ❾. Follow

SIGHTS & HIGHLIGHTS

Qianmen (p30)
Mao Zedong Mausoleum (p37)
Tiananmen Square (p33)
Monument to the People's Heroes
  (p30)
Great Hall of the People (p29)
Tiananmen (p7)
Forbidden City (p8)
Jingshan Park (p32)
Beihai Park (p18)

Strolling through the Forbidden City

the tree-lined trail to the top of the hill for views of the golden palace rooftops to the south and Beihai Park to the northwest. Take the east exit out of the park and walk south to the moat. Cross over Wusi Dajie ❿ and follow it east to the pedestrian path between Beiheyan Dajie ⓫ and Donghuangchenggen Nanjie ⓬. As you head south, join families and exercising grannies out for a twilight stroll. Take a right at Donghuamen Dajie ⓭ to The Courtyard ⓮ (p70) for fine dining with a view over the moat.

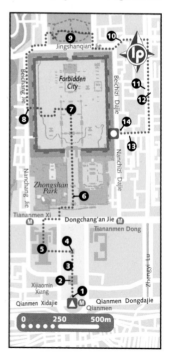

distance 6km **duration** 5hrs
▶ start Ⓜ Qianmen
● end 🚌 60 to Tiananmen Dong

Shoppers' Shuffle

Wander up one side of Liulichang Xijie ❶ and down the other before crossing the bridge to Liulichang Dongjie ❷, a treasure-trove of history. Stop in at Beijing Songtangzhai Museum ❸ to see carving at its best, and then hang a left. Take the second right, just past the vegie market, to a pretty residential *hutong*. Take the second right (where this *hutong* merges with another) and then the first right again. Heading north along this busy street will bring you to the pedestrianised Dazhalan Jie ❹. If you think this is crowded, wait until you take the last left before Qianmen Dajie; a manic, narrow market street. Shuffle north among the crowds and you'll come out at Qianmen ❺. Take the pedestrian underpass and walk through the enormous gate. After a couple more pedestrian underpasses you'll find yourself on a shady sidewalk with views across Tiananmen Square ❻. Head north to the Chinese Revolution & History Museum ❼, take another underpass and enter the serene Workers' Cultural Palace ❽. Rest for a bit in the pavilions before taking the east exit and walking south to the beautiful courtyard of the Imperial Archives and Wan Fung Art Gallery ❾. Walk east along Dongchang'an Jie ❿ and take a left into the shopping oasis of Wangfujing Dajie ⓫. Take the second left, which leads into a narrow *hutong*, and then the first right into what appears to be a courtyard – this winding *hutong* leads north to Wangfujing Snack Street ⓬ (p72), where you can fill up on an exotic dinner-on-a-stick.

distance 5km **duration** 4hrs
▶ start Ⓜ Hepingmen, then any bus south
● end 🚌 Wangfujing

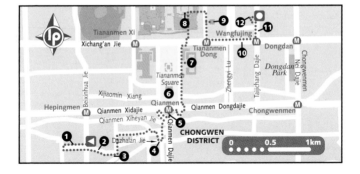

DAY TRIPS
The Great Wall of China at Badaling (1, C2 & 2)

Twisting and turning for more than 5000km and visible from space, you could once traverse the Great Wall from Shanhai Pass on the east coast to Jiayu Pass in the Gobi Desert. While much of the wall has since crumbled or been blown to dust by the wind, a number of sections have been restored and opened to the public.

INFORMATION
70km northwest of Beijing
- Tour Bus 1 from Qianmen
- 6912 1338/1423
- 8.50am-8pm
- Y45/25, plus Y1 insurance (includes entry to the Great Wall Museum and Great Wall Circle Vision Theatre)

The ancient Chinese fortified their cities and states with enormous walls, and by 290BC these walls dotted the country's northern border. When the Mongolian nomadic peoples of the northern plains began to pose a threat to the ambitious and tyrannical Emperor Qin (221-207BC), he indentured thousands of labourers to link the existing walls. For 10 years these labourers toiled and by 214BC the wall was the largest defence mechanism the world had ever seen.

However, by the time of the Sui dynasty (AD589-1279) the wall was a crumbling mess. One million peasants were conscripted to restore it and the harsh conditions they endured resulted in serious uprisings. To add to the Sui's problems, the lengthy wall was difficult to man properly and, seeing their moment, the Mongols swept into China, establishing a capital in present-day Beijing within the shade of the wall that was originally built to keep them out. Years later, the Mings decided to overhaul the once-again-decaying wall, this time with the aid of bricks and stone slabs. Phenomenal amounts of resources and labour were used in the process, but a century later the wall was again in a state of disrepair.

Of course, this isn't to say that the wall was built in vain. It was the linchpin in unifying China and became an excellent thoroughfare for transporting people and equipment across the mountains. By way of its beacon tower system, wolf-dung smoke signals quickly sent news of enemy movement back to the capital. In 1972 US president Richard Nixon visited the wall

Great Wall Recipe
Mix 180 million cu metres of earth with tamarisk twigs and reeds. Press into desired shape, alternating with 7cm to 10cm layers of coarse gravel and clay (can be substituted for other materials at hand, such as deceased labourers). Allow to settle for 1500 to 1600 years. Garnish with 60 million cu metres of bricks and stone slabs, covering the sides and top completely. Serves 1.3 billion.

and commented, 'It sure is a great wall.' Beijing's tourism industry hasn't been the same since.

The easiest place to experience the Great Wall is at **Badaling**. This section of the wall was last restored in 1957. At an elevation of 1000m, it affords some magnificent views of the masonry snaking its way through the mountains and gives you an inkling of the wall's enormity. The

The Great Wall at Badaling

restored section crawls for about 1km each way; head left up the stairs (south) for the vaguely quieter route. It's worth hiking all the way to the end to see the rather forlorn ruins that carry on over the hill. Good footwear is a must.

There's no denying that Badaling is swarming with tourists, and vendors who are convinced that everyone needs an 'I Climbed the Great Wall' T-shirt. This is, after all, one of the world's top tourist destinations and you don't come here for serenity but rather the overwhelming 'I am standing on the Great Wall' sensation. If you really can't face the hubbub, try visiting in the evening when most tours have left, or head to the somewhat quieter 4.5km stretch of the wall between the crazily steep **Simatai** section (1, B5; ☎ 6903 5025; 8am-5pm) and the less-developed **Jinshanling** (1, B5).

Ming Tombs   (1, C2)

In many cultures, the rituals surrounding death play an important role. For emperors of the Ming dynasty (1368-1644), these ceremonies often reached epic proportions, as did the wealth and attention spent on tombs. In this 40-sq-km area, 13 of the 16 Ming emperors were buried with their wives, concubines and funerary treasures. All of the tombs have been plundered in the past but, following recent restorations, three have been opened to the public.

Chang Ling, the resting place of Emperor Yongle, has huge *nanmu* halls and displays of unearthed jewellery and clothing. This tomb is the most impressive of the three; it took 18 years to complete and, according to legend, 16 concubines were buried alive with Yongle's corpse. At **Ding Ling**, the tomb of Emperor Wan Li, you can walk through the underground passageways and caverns. These are mainly giant empty rooms, but the imposing marble doors within the tomb are amazing. **Zhao Ling**, where Emperor Longqing rests, is smaller and relatively tranquil. Leading up to the tombs, **Spirit Way** passes a giant tortoise bearing the largest stele in China, followed by 12 sets of fantastic stone animals and 12 stone-faced statues of generals, ministers and officials. Every other animal is in a reclining position, allowing for a 'changing of the guard' at midnight. The 7km Spirit Way is fabulous and well worth encouraging speed-happy tour bus drivers to stop for a look.

INFORMATION
50km northwest of Beijing

🚌 Tour Bus 1 from Qianmen; or No 845 from Beijing North (Xizhimen) subway to Changping, then taxi 10mins

☎ 6976 1156/1334

ⓘ audio guide Y10/30 Chinese/English (available at Ding Ling), plus Y200 deposit

⌚ 8am-5.30pm

$ Y30-50/tomb; Y20 Spirit Way

Marco Polo Bridge (1, D2 & 3, K1)

Built in 1189, Beijing's oldest marble bridge spans 266m across the Yongding River and is host to 501 uniquely carved stone lions. If you wander along the riverbank, you can get a good view of its 11 arches. En route to the bridge, you'll pass through the ancient city walls of **Wanping** (3, K1).

While enshrined in the travel logs of the great Italian traveller, the bridge is most famous for the Marco Polo Bridge Incident of 1937, when Japanese troops illegally occupied a railway junction outside Wanping. Gunfire was exchanged (it's still possible to find shell pits in Wanping's city walls) and Japan had its pretext for attacking Beijing and igniting a full-scale war.

> ## INFORMATION
> *17km southwest from central Beijing*
> 🚍 964 from Beijing West train station
> ✉ 88 Lugouqiaochengnei Xijie, Wanping
> ☎ 8389 3919
> ⏱ 7am-7pm
> 💲 Y10/5

Nearby, the **Memorial Hall of the War of Resistance** (3, K1) and the **Commemorative Sculpture Garden** (3, K2) will intrigue history buffs.

Bored? Try counting all 501 feisty felines on Marco Polo Bridge

Tanzhe Temple (1, D2)

Beijing's oldest and largest temple reclines amid ancient silver apricot trees, gingkos and towering pines. Dating back to the 3rd century AD, its great age graces the temple with unique features – dragon decorations, mythical animal sculptures and grimacing gods that are no longer found in temples within the city. Locals have traditionally come to this atmospheric retreat to pray for rain during droughts or to harvest Cudrania trees, which provide yellow dye and nourish silkworms.

> **INFORMATION**
>
> *45km west of Beijing*
> - Ⓜ Pingguoyuan, then bus 931 or taxi
> - 🚍 Tour Bus 7 from Qianmen (Apr-Oct Sat-Sun & holidays departs 7-8.30am)
> - 🕑 Apr–mid-Sept 8am-6pm, mid-Sept–Mar 8.20am-4.30pm
> - 💲 Y30/15

Today, the temple grounds retain a calm, spiritual feel. Within the complex, look for the unusual **Tree of Prosperity**, which you can lean on for good luck; the smoky **Guanyin Cave**, where you can taste eternal springwater tea; and the **Stone Fish**, apparently given to the temple by Jade Emperor himself. Outside the temple grounds, **Talin Temple** has a gorgeous collection of intricately detailed stupas.

Chuandixia Village (1, D1)

Nestled in a green valley and overlooked by towering peaks, Chuandixia is an enchanting village forgotten by time. Its cluster of traditional courtyard homes, terraced orchards and beautiful stone alleyways make it a picturesque day trip into rural China. The tiny community has formed a kind of tourism cooperative. In exchange for the small entrance fee to the village, you can have a look inside many of the courtyard buildings (marked with red numbers).

> **INFORMATION**
>
> *90km west of Beijing*
> - Ⓜ Pingguoyuan, then bus 929 to Zhaitang; or taxi (Y80 from Pingguoyuan)
> - 💲 Y20

The money raised appears to be going back into the village, restoring buildings and improving the roads.

As you wander up and around the narrow alleyways, you will likely encounter Maoist graffiti left over from Cultural Revolution days. Slogans such as 'Arm our minds with Mao Zedong Thought' and 'Proletariats of the world unite!' decorate the walls.

You won't find a vendor or a single shop in this peaceful hamlet, as the villagers continue to go about their days grinding corn or picking apples. There's a small teashop up the hill at the far northern end of the village but you'd be wise to bring along your own water and snacks.

ORGANISED TOURS

The Chinese government does its best to keep a firm grip on the tourism industry, largely through its incarnation as the China Travel Service (CTS). CTS runs half- and full-day tours around Beijing but they are generally uninspired and often include stops at government-operated shops and restaurants. Unfortunately, there isn't a flood of other options to choose from. Included here are a few companies, mainly operating at large hotels. You're also likely to be approached by 'tour guides' on the street – many offer excellent, personalised tours at good rates, however, be warned that there is always the risk of fraud and theft involved.

Beijing Tourist Hutong Agency (4, C5)
In addition to popular, guided rickshaw tours of Beijing's *hutongs*, the 'Learn to be a Beijinger' tour gives you a chance to learn how to make (and eat!) dumplings in a traditional courtyard home.
✉ 26 Di'anmen Xidajie ☎ 6615 9097, 6612 3236
🕙 8.50am/1.50pm morning/afternoon tour
💲 from Y190

China Travel Service
(3, D13) CTS runs convoys of bus tours to Beijing's biggest sights, including the Great Wall, Ming Tombs, Forbidden City, Temple of Heaven and to opera and acrobatic performances. The tours are often geared towards Chinese tourists and guides don't always speak English. Tour groups tend to be large and schedules tight. Reserve one day in advance.
✉ 2 Beisanhuan Donglu; offices in large hotels, incl Holiday Inn, Novotel & Hilton
☎ 6464 6400 ext 6448/6422 🕙 tours vary
💲 Y350-415

Dragon Bus (4, H8)
Dragon Bus offers tours to the expected sights, catering to business tour groups and offering pre- and post-conference tours.
✉ Beijing Hotel, 33 Dongchang'an Jie
☎ 6513 7766 ext 1850
🕙 most tours daily
💲 Y350-380

Hello Beijing (4, K5)
Focusing on the *hutongs* of Qianmen, this rickshaw tour takes in a kindergarten, a family courtyard home, markets and the Zhengyi Ci Theatre. Book a day in advance to ensure an English-speaking guide and two days in advance if you'd like lunch provided.
✉ 13 Danlanying Hutong ☎ 6302 7010
🕙 9am, 2pm & 7pm
💲 from Y230

Panda Tour (3, G8)
With smaller tour groups and English-speaking guides, this is a good alternative to CTS. Tours visit popular Beijing sights, *hutongs*, acrobatic performances and the Mutianyu section of the Great Wall. There are also day trips to Chengde and three-day tours to Xi'an.
✉ 36 Nanlishi Lu; counters at St Regis, Kempinski, Jinglun & Shangri-la Hotels
☎ 6803 6963
🕙 most tours daily; Mutianyu Great Wall: Sunday 💲 Y260-390 incl lunch

River Romance (4, C6)
Candlelit boat tours around Houhai and Qianhai Lakes in a private, Chinese-style gondola. A musician in the bow strumming traditional music adds to the exotic atmosphere.
✉ southern end of Qianhai Lake, off Di'anmen Xidajie
☎ 6612 5717
🕙 9am-10pm (evenings best) 💲 Y180/70mins, plus Y100 for live music

Tour guide wields his weapon to round up the stragglers

Shopping

Beijingers have burst out of their navy Mao suits and have taken to the malls. Shopping has become a lucrative linchpin in the capital's economic growth and a major pastime, with hard-nosed consumers pounding the pavements morning, noon and night. You can't blame them – the shopping here is tops, with everything from the dazzle of Tiffany's to the hustle of the Silk Market. The real finds are at the antique markets, where discerning eyes can unearth gems.

Shopping Areas

The pedestrianised, southern end of **Wangfujing** is *the* place to shop for name-brand goods, with **Jianguomen Wai Dajie** following closely. **Sanlitun** and the streets around the **Workers' Stadium** are where the smaller, trendy designer shops are springing up, while **Qianmen** has some of Beijing's oldest outlets for silk and tea and is packed with clothing stalls. **Xidan Beidajie** is where young people conglomerate en masse and shop and shop and shop...

Opening Hours

To keep up with their customers' spending sprees, closing time is fading further into the night. Most malls and chain shops are open seven days a week, from 9am or 10am until 10pm, as are many of the boutiques around Sanlitun.

Paying & Bargaining

Prices are fixed in malls and department stores. Markets, tourist and antique shops are another matter, where bargaining is a time-honoured tradition. You'll quickly know if you've tried bargaining in a fixed-price shop by the disappearing backside of the retailer. In older shops, the exchange of money for goods can be a convoluted process: you point out what you want, are given a ticket to give to a cashier who collects your money and gives you a stamped receipt to return to the salesperson in exchange for your purchase. Got it?

CLOTHING & SHOE SIZES

Women's Clothing

Aust/UK	8	10	12	14	16	18
Europe	36	38	40	42	44	46
Japan	5	7	9	11	13	15
USA	6	8	10	12	14	16

Women's Shoes

Aust/USA	5	6	7	8	9	10
Europe	35	36	37	38	39	40
France only	35	36	38	39	40	42
Japan	22	23	24	25	26	27
UK	3½	4½	5½	6½	7½	8½

Men's Clothing

Aust	92	96	100	104	108	112
Europe	46	48	50	52	54	56

Japan	S		M	M		L
UK/USA	35	36	37	38	39	40

Men's Shirts (Collar Sizes)

Aust/Japan	38	39	40	41	42	43
Europe	38	39	40	41	42	43
UK/USA	15	15½	16	16½	17	17½

Men's Shoes

Aust/ UK	7	8	9	10	11	12
Europe	41	42	43	44½	46	47
Japan	26	27	27.5	28	29	30
USA	7½	8½	9½	10½	11½	12½

Measurements approximate only; try before you buy.

SHOPPING CENTRES & DEPARTMENT STORES

Beijing New World
(4, K9) Kids can play in the jungle gym upstairs or slurp drinks at the juice bar while you shop. Shirts, jewellery, perfume, bread and everything else are well organised in this relatively new multilevel department store.
✉ cnr Chongwenmen Wai Dajie & Dong-damochang Jie
Ⓜ Chongwenmen
🕒 10am-9pm

China World Shopping Centre (4, H15)
Chock-a-block with top, international shops like Christian Dior and Gucci, this hushed and refined mall is for the well-heeled crowd.
✉ 1 Jianguomen Wai Dajie Ⓜ Guo Mao
🕒 9am-10pm

Dongan Department Store & Shopping Centre
(4, G9) Verging on frenzied, this place has a market feel. Lots of material, lots of tailor-made outfits and quite a bit of clutter.
✉ Wangfujing Dajie
Ⓜ Wangfujing
🕒 10am-10pm

The grandiose Oriental Plaza

Friendship Store (4, H13)
If you just can't find the souvenirs you're looking for and don't mind the drab interior, the Friendship Store is an old standby for coffee-table books, fans and trinkets (not to mention Hershey's chocolate and cheddar cheese!).
✉ 17 Jianguomen Wai Dajie Ⓜ Yong An Li
🕒 9am-9pm

Kerry Mall (4, G15)
The deceivingly dreary exterior of this place hides an oasis. Have your hair styled, get aromatherapied-up, sample a fine wine, replace your forgotten stationery, send your postcards, develop your photos and wander through a few quiet boutiques.
✉ Guanghua Lu
Ⓜ Guo Mao, then any bus north 🕒 9am-9pm

One World Department Store (4, F8)
New and elegant, this is where fashion-conscious men can buy top designs from Joseph, Austin Reed and Comme des Garcon.
✉ 99 Wangfujing Dajie
Ⓜ Wangfujing, then bus 101 🕒 10am-9.30pm

Shop till you drop at Dongan

Pacific Department Store

Oriental Plaza (4, H9)
From Nike to Valentino to a range of local boutiques, you'll find it all in Beijing's finest shopping centre. This place is very kid-friendly, with nappy-changing rooms and a playroom downstairs.

✉ 1 Dongchang'an Jie Ⓜ Wangfujing ⏰ 9.30am-10pm

Pacific Department Store (4, C15)
This upmarket store has clothing for all, as well as electronics and cosmetics. There's a pharmacy, laundry and supermarket.

✉ 2 Gongren Tiyuchang Beilu Ⓜ Dongsishitiao, then bus 113 ⏰ 10.30am-10pm

Scitech Plaza (4, H13)
Overflowing and a bit over-crowded with an enormous selection of goods, you can also pick up some groceries or a new hairstyle here.

✉ 22 Jianguomen Wai Dajie Ⓜ Yong An Li ⏰ 10am-9pm

Youyi Lufthansa Centre (3, D13)
One of the city's long-established department stores, it's well stocked with brand-name goods. You'll find Chinese medicine at ground level.

✉ 50 Liangmaqiao Lu Ⓜ Guo Mao, then bus 207 ⏰ 10am-10pm

FOOD & DRINK

CRC Shop (4, H9)
You'll satisfy all your hunger pains at this large, modern grocery store. It's a great place to pick up snacks before heading out on an excursion. It also has a good selection of baby food and bulk loose tea, and there's a small drugstore.

✉ BB01a, Oriental Plaza, 1 Dongchang'an Jie Ⓜ Wangfujing ⏰ 9am-9pm

Hongqiao Market (6, C5)
Scorpions, snake meat, snails – buy Beijing's delicacies in bulk at this frenzied food market.

✉ Basement, 16 Hongqiao Lu Ⓜ Chong-wenmen, then bus 43 ⏰ 8.30am-7pm

Liubiju (4, K6)
This 400-year-old pickle-and-sauce emporium has a fantastic reputation among its clientele of local connoisseurs.

✉ 3 Liangshidian Jie, off Dazhalan Jie Ⓜ Qianmen ⏰ 10am-6pm

Paris Patisserie (4, F13)
Freshly baked bread comes

Liubiju: a pickle-lover's heaven

out of the oven three times a day and is sold alongside Western cakes and cookies, and more-unusual desserts like green-tea mousse.

✉ 1 Ritan Donglu Ⓜ Jianguomen, then bus 29 ⏰ 8am-6pm

Ten Fu's Tea (4, K6)
With branches all over town, this is the place to buy top-quality loose tea from around the country. In the time-honoured tradition, a cup of tea is offered to you as soon as you walk inside the shop, and knowledgeable staff offer free tea-ceremony demonstrations upstairs at the Dazhalan branch. Try some jasmine tea, consisting of buds only, or some black-tea candy for a caffeine buzz.

✉ Dazhalan Jie (northern side) Ⓜ Qian-men ⏰ 10am-7pm

MARKETS

Beijing Curio City (3, J13)
Four floors of scrolls, ceramics, carpets, furniture and duty-free goods. Your trolling will more than likely be rewarded with top knick-knacks and souvenirs.
✉ **21 Dongsanhuan Nanlu** Ⓜ **Guo Mao, then bus 28**
🕑 **9.30am-6.30pm**

Looking for that perfect outfit at Xiushui Silk Market

Hongqiao Market (6, C5)
Freshwater pearls are a great buy in China and the Pearl Market is Beijing's top outlet. There are also vendors selling shoes, electronics, crafts and antiques.
✉ **3rd fl, 16 Hongqiao**

Doing the vogue thing

Lu Ⓜ **Chongwenmen, then bus 43**
🕑 **8.30am-7pm**

Panjiayuan Market (3, J13) It may be known as the Dirt Market but it's the place to shop for arts, crafts, furniture and antiques. Discerning shoppers can pick up some real finds here amongst the family heirlooms carted in each weekend from the countryside. Bright and early Sunday morning is when the pickings are best, but deals are better later in the day.
✉ **Panjiayuan Lu** Ⓜ **Guo Mao, then bus 28** 🕑 **Sat-Sun dawn-3pm**

Xiushui Silk Market (4, H14) Silk galore! Boxer shorts, scarves, shirts, ties, purses and robes line the stalls alongside fake designer goods. Bargaining is a must, and keep your senses and your purse about you – this is pickpocket territory.
✉ **Jianguomen Wai Dajie** Ⓜ **Yong An Li** 🕑 **9am-dusk**

Yabao Market (4, F12)
Rumours of demolition have not yet stopped this hectic Russian market, with its sprawl of fur coats, jewellery and electronics.
✉ **off Ritan Lu** Ⓜ **Jianguomen, then bus 29** 🕑 **9.30am-4pm**

Game Plan
You barely need to glance at an item before the vendor is pulling it off the display and excitedly asking you, 'How much?' Don't get flustered, this is only the first round of bargaining. It's an exhilarating national sport in China and the only real rule (if you want to win) is to be polite. If you're worried about cheating the vendor out of a fair price, don't be – it's nearly impossible. These guys are much better at this game than you, and won't let their goods go for peanuts. As you're expected to bargain, the first price you're offered will be at least double the going rate. Look 'em straight in the eye and cut that number in half. You'll likely end up with something in between. If not, walk away and see what that does to the price.

CLOTHING & ACCESSORIES

Can Cam (4, C15)

Hip fashions from Paris, Italy and Hong Kong. Jeans with lace cuts, shoes with prints and tops with tassels; this is where Daisy Duke's wealthy cousin would shop.

✉ **51 Sanlitun Lu**
Ⓜ **Dongsishitiao,**
then bus 113 or 115
🕐 **10.30am–midnight**

Hiersun Diamond Palace

(4, H9) This luxurious shop sells gorgeous gems, including cases and cases of girls' best friends.

✉ **AA29, Oriental Plaza, 1 Dongchang'an Jie**
Ⓜ **Wangfujing**
🕐 **9.30am–10pm**

Jali Clothes Market

(4, A15) This indoor complex has a dizzying array of stalls selling fake designer goods, sunglasses, bags, shoes and Gore-Tex jackets.

✉ **across from Kunlun Hotel, Xinyuan Nanlu**
Ⓜ **Dongzhimen, then bus 24** 🕐 **9.30am–9pm**

Jam Jam (4, C14)

This shop carries chic clothing with traditional Chinese flair. The in-house designer does alterations and can whip up one of her

Jackets at Jam Jam

displayed designs in a different colour.

✉ **alley off cnr Gongren Tiyuchang Beilu & Gongrentiyuguan Donglu**
Ⓜ **Dongsishitiao, then bus 113** 🕐 **10am–11pm**

Sanlitun Yashou Clothing Market (4, C14)

Innumerable stalls of traditional, outdoor and trendy clothes, hats and shoes can be found inside this new five-storey complex. There are some good deals to be bargained for. The fantastic food court upstairs is a good place to rest your shopping-weary legs.

✉ **58 Gongren Tiyuchang Beilu**
Ⓜ **Dongsishitiao, then bus 113** 🕐 **9.30am–9pm**

Shanghai Tang (4, H15)

These ultra-chic, Hong Kong designs have made it to the runways of Milan. *Qipaos* and scholars' jackets have been rejuvenated with funky fabrics.

✉ **L203A, Tower A, China World Shopping Centre, 1 Jianguomen Wai Dajie** Ⓜ **Guo Mao**
🕐 **10am–9pm**

SZBR Culture & Art Dress Shop (4, C14)

Handmade by a local designer, the women's clothing here is casual and

modern and much of it has an ethnic feel to it. The shop is set back from the street; look for a bright blue speech bubble above the door.

✉ **12 Gongren Tiyuchang Beilu**
Ⓜ **Dongsishitiao, then bus 113** 🕐 **10am–10pm**

Yan Jing Cheng Eyeglass City (3, J13)

This wholesale supply store has every colour, shape and size of frame as well as heaps of name-brand knockoffs and lots of deals. Within an hour you can have your eyes examined (Y10) and prescription lenses fitted and tinted. Head for stall D19.

✉ **64 Dongsanhuan Nanlu** Ⓜ **Guo Mao, then bus 28** 🕐 **8am–7pm**

Yo Yo (4, C15)

This shop offers distinctive, semi-bold clothing and accessories for women. The sales assistants are helpfully nonpushy.

✉ **30 Sanlitun Lu**
Ⓜ **Dongsishitiao, then bus 113** 🕐 **10am–11.30pm**

Window shopping at SZBR

TAILORS

Cao Senlin (4, F10)
This lovely and extremely talented man has been designing and hand-sewing *qipaos* since 1938. He's one of the few traditional *qipao* makers left in the city. His workshop is in his small courtyard home. Bring your own material and, if you don't speak Chinese, a translator too. Dresses take about three weeks.

✉ **25 Shijia Hutong (1st door on left through corridor)** ☎ **6526 4515** Ⓜ **Dongdan, then any bus north** ⏱ **hit-and-miss; call ahead**

Dreamweavers (4, A14)
Designers here can whip you up a contemporary, funky *qipao* in about a week.

✉ **51 Taiyuancun Lu** Ⓜ **Dongzhimen, then bus 206 or 403** ⏱ **10am-6pm**

Mu Zhen Lao (4, G9)
One of Beijing's most famous *qipao* makers has racks of dresses for sale. If you can't find anything quite right among these traditional and stylish designs, you can have something tailored in a couple of weeks.

✉ **shop 246 Shandong'an Plaza, 138 Wangfujing Dajie** Ⓜ **Wangfujing** ⏱ **10am-9pm**

Mushi
Caroline Deleens has blazed onto the Beijing fashion scene. Her fashions are a mixture of French and Chinese fabrics and styles – unusual but wearable off the runway. To see her collections, call for an appointment.

☎ **1370 111 4361**

Wuzhou Friendship Silk Trade Company (4, B14)
Favoured by expats for quality work at reasonable rates, this no-frills shop has reams of material to choose from. *Qipaos* can be made in three to four days and suits in a week.

✉ **2nd fl, Friendship Supermarket, 7 Sanlitun Lu** Ⓜ **Dongzhimen, then bus 117 or 206** ⏱ **10am-7pm**

Yanhuiyuan Fashion (4, C14)
You can buy material from this shop or one of the many surrounding stalls. Dresses and suits can be tailored for you in a few days. The styles aren't too flashy, but classy all the same.

✉ **3rd fl, Sanlitun Yashou Clothing Market, Gongren Tiyuchang Beilu** Ⓜ **Dongsishitiao, then bus 113** ⏱ **9.30am-9pm**

Yongzheng Tailor (4, F9)
Much of what's in stock is garish, but there are some exquisite embroidered jackets and the friendly staff can tailor dresses and men's suits in a couple of weeks.

✉ **cnr Wangfujing Dajie & Dengshikou Jie** Ⓜ **Wangfujing, then bus 101** ⏱ **10am-8pm**

Dress to Impress
With its narrow cut and high 'mandarin' collar, the *qipao* is the most easily recognised traditional Chinese outfit. In the days of Qing royalty and Manchu nobility it was all the rage, before men went the way of trousers and women transformed the *qipao* into an elegant frock. Apart from a brief Mao-pantsuit glitch, the *qipao* has remained a staple in women's closets ever since. These days they've raised the hemline, turned up the volume on the material and made the *qipao* chic all over again. You'll find them hanging in market stalls, department stores and designer shops, or you can get a perfect fit at a tailor.

ARTS & CRAFTS

Beijing Arts & Crafts Central Store (4, H9)
This place is particularly well known for its jade and jadeite, but the selection here is far better than the prices.
✉ 200 Wangfujing Dajie Ⓜ Wangfujing
🕑 10am-9pm

Think domestic at Home Store Design

Home Store Design
(4, C14) Vibrant silk curtains, ceramic plates with unique glazes, inspired lamps and rugged pottery fill this tiny shop. All are original pieces and most are the creation of designer Cui Rui.
✉ Gongren Tiyuchang Beilu Ⓜ Dongsishitiao, then bus 113
🕑 9am-10pm

Made In Paradise (4, K6)
With incense sticks burning up a storm and prayer bells ringing, you can almost imagine yourself in Tibet. The Indo-Tibetan arts and crafts sold here include music and jewellery.
✉ 41 Dazhalan Jie
Ⓜ Qianmen
🕑 10am-7pm

Metis (4, C14)
Gorgeous! This small shop sells handmade bedspreads, embroidered pillowcases, linen sets, lamps and curtains. Quilt and pillowcase sets come in a matching carry bag. The designers have a reputation for being easy to work with and will tailor pieces for you.
✉ 6 Gongren Tiyuchang Beilu Ⓜ Dongsishitiao, then bus 113
🕑 9am-6pm

Rongbaozhai (4, K4)
Although the interior of this shop may not inspire you to use them, paper, ink and brushes have long been sold here. There's an excellent selection of scrolls, paintings and wood blocks.
✉ 19 Liulichang Xijie
Ⓜ Hepingmen, then any bus south 🕑 10am-6pm

Tumasek (4, H9)
Beautiful, gleaming goblets, trays, jugs and decanters made of Malaysian pewter; a little heavy to lug home but totally unique.
✉ A108, Oriental Plaza, 1 Dongchang'an Jie
Ⓜ Wangfujing
🕑 9.30am-10pm

Valiante & Leisure National Handicraft Store (4, C14)
Rows of beaded shoes, plush woven carpets and intricate bronze carvings fill this atmospheric, Pakistani store.
✉ west off Sanlitun Lu
Ⓜ Dongsishitiao, then bus 113 🕑 10am-10pm

Zen Cat Gallery (4, B6)
Stepping onto the mosaic-tiled patio, you will immediately see that this gallery is unique. Dong Zi is a growing sensation on the Beijing art scene and her creations, which fill this small room, will show you why. Very imaginative work at reasonable prices. Opening hours are a bit hit-and-miss.
✉ 14 Houhai Nanyun
☎ 6651 5392 🚌 5, 58, 210 🕑 9-10am & noon-1pm

All That Glitters
For aspiring artists there is a time-honoured Chinese tradition of learning by imitating the works of masters. These days they're going so far as to hone the masters' signature, too. In Panjiayuan Market it is estimated that 99% of the paintings and calligraphy by big-name artists are fakes. Not too surprising if you consider that paintings by Qi Gong, going for Y60 at the market, are worth over Y100,000. To quote a stall owner: 'If I had an authentic painting by one of those artists, just one, would I stay here?'

MUSIC & BOOKS

Music comes to you in Beijing. Walk down Jianguomen Wai Dajie or Sanlitun Lu and you'll be approached by street vendors murmuring 'CD? VCD?' and carrying bags full of them. Copyright laws are nowhere to be seen in Beijing, so pirated copies of popular (and not so popular) CDs are mass-produced. China's entry into the World Trade Organization was partly conditional on the trade being cleaned up, but no-one seems to have told the CD vendors.

Audio Visual World
(4, K7) Western pop music and classical Chinese meet on these shelves. Nothing too unusual but lots to choose from.
✉ Qianmen Dajie, just south of Dazhalan Jie
Ⓜ Qianmen
🕑 9am-10pm

A good map of Beijing will go a long way...

China Bookstore (4, K5)
Everything here is in Chinese, but the antiquarian books make for some interesting browsing, as do the stacks of art books.
✉ 115 Liulichang Dongjie Ⓜ Hepingmen, then any bus south
🕑 10am-6pm

Cool Music World (4, G9)
Craving some Western music? Come here and have a listen before you buy. CDs are a steal.
✉ Dongdan Beidajie
Ⓜ Dongdan
🕑 9am-9pm

Foreign Languages Bookshop (4, G8)
If you've finished your novel or are looking for bedtime stories for the kids, head here. There's also a small selection of English-language travel books if you plan to head further afield.
✉ 235 Wangfujing Dajie Ⓜ Wangfujing, then bus 101
🕑 10am-6pm

Lao She Former Residence (4, F8)
Rickshaw Boy, *Cat City* and *Tea House* are all available in Chinese and English from the author's former home.
✉ 19 Fengfu Hutong
Ⓜ Wangfujing, then bus 2, 52 or 210
🕑 Tues-Sun 9am-4pm

Wangfujing Bookshop
(4, H9) Huge and teeming

All shopped out?

A map seller sets up shop in a pedestrian underpass

with shoppers, this is a good place to buy maps of the city and beyond. There is also a very small selection of fairly mundane English fiction on the 4th floor.
✉ **218 Wangfujing Dajie** Ⓜ **Wangfujing** ⌚ **10am-9pm**

World of Books (3, D13)
Quite a few Lonely Planet titles (never miss a plug!) and photographic coffee-table books on Beijing and China. There is also a small selection for kids and a few classic English novels.
✉ **6th fl, Youyi Lufthansa Centre, 50 Liangmaqiao Lu** Ⓜ **Guo Mao, then bus 207** ⌚ **10am-10pm**

Xidan Bookshop (4, H3)
Large, but largely Chinese. There are a few English-language books on the 3rd floor but nothing to get too excited about.
✉ **17 Xichang'an Jie** Ⓜ **Xidan** ⌚ **10am-7pm**

Yin Xiang Chao Shin (4, C14) A good selection of Chinese pop, some old stuff for Goth fans, R&B and some one-off compilations by Western groups like Blur. It's open late and worth a browse if you're in the neighbourhood.
✉ **Gongren Tiyuchang Beilu** Ⓜ **Dongsishitiao, then bus 113** ⌚ **11am-late**

'Read All About It!'

There is enough literature on China to see you through the next millennium. Strangely, there's barely enough on Beijing to see you through your flight. In Beijing itself, you can find English copies of *Rickshaw Boy*, a window into the living conditions of rickshaw drivers in the early 20th century. *Dragon Lady: The Life & Legend of the Last Empress of China* by Sterling Seagrave is the fascinating biography of Cixi (see p13). *Twilight in the Forbidden City* is by Reginald F Johnston and describes his days tutoring the last emperor of China. *Foreign Mud* by Maurice Collins discusses the opium trade and ensuing Opium Wars. *The Siege at Peking* by Peter Fleming is an excellent account of the Boxer Rebellion in Beijing, while *The Tiananmen Papers* blows away the official smokescreen hanging over 4 June 1989.

FOR CHILDREN

Children are probably the easiest people to buy souvenirs for in Beijing – mini-parasols, fabulous kites and child-size *qipaos* and scholars' jackets are for sale at most markets and at lots of tourist sights. Also try the many shops just southwest of Qianmen Gate.

Honey World (4, H9)
A children's mini-mall within a mall that sells picture books, bright clothing and plush toys.
✉ Basement, Oriental Plaza, 1 Dongchang'an Jie
Ⓜ Wangfujing
🕑 9.30am-10pm

Jali Clothes Market
(4, A15) In the back right corner of this market you'll find stalls selling original and not so original brand-name clothing for kids, as well as toys and shoes. The Baby Mexx stall has the best selection.
✉ across from Kunlun Hotel, Xinyuan Nanlu
Ⓜ Dongzhimen, then bus 24
🕑 9.30am-9pm

Kaixinbaobao (4, D13)
Forgotten a baby essential like food, formula, nappies, bottles, educational toys, clothes or even the stroller? This orderly baby-supply shop can sell you whatever you need.
✉ Workers' Stadium (west entrance), Gongren Tiyuchang Xilu Ⓜ Dong-sishitiao, then any bus east 🕑 9am-7pm

Kid's World (3, D13)
This is a fashion-conscious kid's paradise. You'll find miniature-sized *qipaos* and scholars' jackets as well as imports from Hong Kong and Europe.
✉ 2nd fl, Youyi Lufthansa Centre, 50 Liangmaqiao Lu

Ⓜ Guo Mao, then bus 207 🕑 10am-10pm

New China Children's Toy World (4, G9)
'Bleep! Whrrrrr . . . Tweet!' After a trip to this maze of whirling toys, gadgets, flashing lights and electronic noises, you may be deaf and your kids will be giddy.
✉ Wangfujing Dajie
Ⓜ Wangfujing
🕑 10am-8pm

New China Children's Toy World mascot

ANTIQUES

The best haunt for antique shoppers is Panjiayuan Market (p55).

Cottage (4, F13)
Among the modern interior decor you'll find fantastic antique Buddha chests,

cabinets, furniture, screens, jewellery cases and carvings. A very pleasant and relaxed shopping experience.
✉ 4 Ritan Beilu
Ⓜ Jianguomen, then bus 29 🕑 10am-8.30pm

Yidege (4, K5)
You've been able to buy liquid Indian inks here since 1865. Today it's also a treasure chest of antique carvings, scrolls and porcelain. Use

discriminating eyes.
✉ 67 Liulichang Dongjie Ⓜ Hepingmen, then any bus south
🕑 10am-6pm

Yihong Carpet Factory
(6, C5) This small, dusty warehouse has stacks of antique carpets from around China and Tibet. It's a bit disorganised but worth the dig.
✉ 35 Juzhang Lu
Ⓜ Chongwenmen, then bus 41 🕑 10am-6pm

SPECIALIST STORES

Daiyuexuan Brush Shop
(4, K5) Since 1916 this shop has been perfecting the art of producing sharp-nibbed weasel- and goat-hair brushes. You can also buy rice paper, ink and ink stones. Now all you need is the calligraphy skills.
✉ **73 Liulichang Dongjie** Ⓜ **Hepingmen**, then any bus south ⏱ 10am-6pm

Dining Room (3, E14)
Everything you need to host a chic Chinese banquet in the comfort of your own dining room. Silk and linen napkins, tablecloths and placemats, original Chinese-knot napkin holders, chopsticks and a fantastic selection of traditional and modern Chinese crockery. It'll make your Chinese take-out look fab.
✉ **Chaoyang Amusement Park (east gate)** Ⓜ **Dongsishitiao**, then bus 115 ⏱ 10am-midnight

Herborist (4, H9)
The package says 'a modern

interpretation of Chinese herbs' – whatever it is, these bath oils, foot scrubs, facial masks and creams smell divine. And the shop is so calm it feels like therapy just stepping inside.
✉ **CJ67, Oriental Plaza, 1 Dongchang'an Jie** Ⓜ **Wangfujing** ⏱ 9.30am-10pm

Jiangnan Silk World
(4, C14) Specialising in double-faced silk embroidery from Suzhou, you can find gorgeous pure-silk quilts, carpets and clothes as well as a loom and a few friendly silk worms on display.
✉ **Workers' Stadium (north entrance), Gongren Tiyuchang Beilu**

Ⓜ **Dongsishitiao**, then any bus east ⏱ 11am-7pm

Nanyang Mannequins & Hangers (4, G8)
Hoping for an ideal or even impossibly shaped body? You can pick one up here. True, some are missing their heads, others their legs. In the end, you're unlikely to actually make a purchase in this shop, but it's worth a look just for its bizarreness. The staff aren't much friendlier than the mannequins.
✉ **52 Donghuamen Dajie** Ⓜ **Wangfujing** ⏱ 9am-5pm

Pipe's Café (4, D14)
For those in need of a quality fix, you can pick up classic pipes, over 60 blends of tobacco and 20 types of cigars here.
✉ **Workers' Stadium (south entrance), Gongren Tiyuchang Nanlu** Ⓜ **Dongsishitiao**, then bus 118 ⏱ 2pm-late

Quintero Tobacco & Wine (4, G15)
Pick up your favourite cigars and sample a 1989 Chateau Lafite Rothschild (Y5800) while you're at it.
✉ **Shop 121, Kerry Centre, 1 Guanghua Lu** Ⓜ **Guo Mao**, then any bus north ⏱ noon-6pm

Ruifuxiang (4, K6)
Even if you're not interested in textiles, this century-old shop is worth a browse for its incredible selection of

What's the Difference?

Watch that newly purchased *qipao* (traditional Chinese outfit) with hawk-like eyes as it journeys from the salesgirl's hands to the bag, lest you get back to your hotel room and discover it has transformed itself into a moth-eaten mess. Shop assistants have been known to switch purchases for damaged goods, and getting a refund, exchange or confession out of them is as easy as finding a seat on the bus in rush hour. Be ruthless in checking your change as well – counterfeit money is rife in Beijing and foreigners are prime targets.

Shandong silk, brocade and satin-silk. The brocade silks are woven with traditional designs of dragons, bamboo and the *shou* (long-life) symbol.

✉ 5 Dazhalan Xijie
Ⓜ Qianmen
🕑 10am-6pm

Wande Photo Equipment (4, D9)

A wander through this shop is like a lesson in the history of photography. You can get practically any photographic equipment or service here, and can browse through a large collection of coffee-table photography books.

✉ 35 Cui Fu Jia Dao
Ⓜ Dongdan, then bus 116 🕑 9am-6pm

Xie Xian Shun (4, K5)

Known as chops, stamps are still commonly used throughout China in place of signatures. You'll see their inky effect on paintings and official documents. The shelves are loaded with jade, marble and stone chops; pick one and have your name carved on it in two minutes flat.

✉ 107b Liulichang Dongjie Ⓜ Hepingmen, then any bus south
🕑 10am-6pm

Xing Haiyuexuan Musical Instruments

(4, K5) If you're not a fan of traditional Chinese music you'll likely find the instruments easier on the eyes than the ears. Beautiful *erhu*

(fiddles), *guzheng* (zithers) and *pipas* (lutes) are sold here. One of the owners gives short demonstrations on the different instruments and, if you do make a purchase, she also gives lessons for Y100/hr.

✉ 97 Liulichang Dongjie
Ⓜ Hepingmen, then any bus south 🕑 10am-6pm

Zhaojia Chaowai Market (3, J13)

Here you'll find loads of traditional Chinese furniture, from opium beds to barrel-stools. Many stall owners claim their wares date back to the Qing and Ming dynasties – highly unlikely, but prices are reasonable.

✉ 43 Huawei Beilu
Ⓜ Guo Mao, then bus 28

SPORTS & OUTDOOR EQUIPMENT

Beijing Hongshang Golf Pro Shop (4, A15)

This place has everything you need to get you ready for the green.

✉ 8 Xinyuan Nanlu
Ⓜ Dongzhimen, then bus 24 🕑 9.30am-9.30pm

Beijing North Huao Sports (4, F8)

A vast selection covering sports such as badminton, baseball, basketball, table tennis, darts and boxing.

✉ Wangfujing Dajie
Ⓜ Wangfujing
🕑 10am-8pm

Extreme Beyond (4, D14)

Looking for the right footwear to scale the Great Wall? This small shop has a good selection of hiking boots,

water-proof jackets, backpacks and sleeping bags (just in case you miss the bus back).

✉ 6 Gongrentiyuguan Donglu Ⓜ Dongsishitiao, then any bus east
🕑 10am-6pm

King Camp (4, D13)

King Camp lives up to his name, with excellent jackets, footwear and tents.

✉ Workers' Stadium (north entrance), Gongren Tiyuchang Beilu Ⓜ Dongsishitiao, then any bus east 🕑 9am-9pm

Sport 100 (4, H9)

This place has everything for those who play sports, and clothes for those who like to look like they do.

Sport 100

✉ AA67, Oriental Plaza, 1 Dongchang'an Jie
Ⓜ Wangfujing
🕑 9.30am-10pm

Tennis Fan (4, C6)

All manner of tennis wares are packed into this hole-in-the-wall shop.

✉ across from Beihai Park (north gate), Di'anmen Xidajie 🚌 5, 111, 118 🕑 10am-7pm

Eating

As you squeeze onto a local bus, relax under a tree in the park or whiz past a group of people on your bike, you'll be met by the same greeting: '*Chi fanle ma?*' ('Have you eaten rice yet?'). Food is never far from the minds of Chinese people and eating is the most social activity in town.

Cuisines

Chinese cuisine is divided into four main schools, one for each compass point. While you'll encounter incarnations of them all here, Beijing traditionally subscribes to the northern school. Wheat or millet was originally much more abundant than rice, hence the popularity of *shunjuyan* (spring rolls) and *jiaozi* (steamed dumplings). Beijing's (and China's) most famous dish, *Beijing kaoya* (Peking duck), is served with typical northern ingredients: wheat pancakes, spring onions and fermented bean paste.

The main methods of northern cooking are steaming, baking and hotpot – a leftover from the Mongols. 'Explode-frying' (deep-frying) came into use due to the scarcity of fuel and later to take advantage of the profusion of peanut oil.

With its fertile soil and coastline, the eastern school abounds with fish and fresh vegetables. This is where the archetypal 'stir-fry' originates. The western school, particularly Sichuan food, is known to burn your pants off with its red chilli and flower pepper (try some almond milk to cool the fires).

Further south, the food is much more exotic – there's a saying that the only four-legged thing these people won't eat is the table. Dogs, cats, monkeys and rats all find their way into the pot. Food preparation is far more complex in these parts, and it's the type of

Meal Costs
The prices listed in this chapter represent the average cost for one person's main course, excluding drinks, starters and desserts.

$	up to Y50
$$	Y51-100
$$$	Y101-150
$$$$	over Y150

Chinese food most commonly found overseas; *dim sum* has become a worldwide, Sunday institution.

Beijing has become truly cosmopolitan in the dining room and you'll be able to satisfy cravings for everything from souvlaki to *yaki soba*. New restaurants are continuously springing up to keep up with the ever more affluent, ever more adventurous, hollow-legged populace.

Etiquette

Dining Chinese-style is a steamy, noisy and often messy affair; nothing like the hushed, candlelit atmosphere of Western dining. Eating out is very communal, with huge groups of people crowded around big, round tables and sharing from the many dishes ordered. Dodge, but think nothing of chicken bones spat on the table or floor – this is very acceptable behaviour. And don't worry about being too tidy as you wield your chopsticks; spillage isn't given a second glance. Tacky-looking restaurants with plastic chairs and tablecloths are sometimes the most popular. Tuck in and find out why – Chinese restaurants' reputations are based solely on the food, not the decor.

In all of this chaos, you might think etiquette went out the window with the leftover chicken feet. *Au contraire.* There are some definite dos and don'ts in Chinese dining. First off, don't pour your own drinks. Pour for your hosts and let them fill your cup, otherwise you insinuate that they're not taking care of you. Try not to ask where the rice is – it's often served after the other dishes and you risk insulting the cook's main courses.

Don't stick your chopsticks into your rice bowl while you reach for something else, as this is reminiscent of an offering to the dead. It's polite to finish your rice, but leaving a bit of the main dishes is okay as it lets your host know that you had enough to eat. Finally, you'll be expected to try to pay, but don't fight too hard. The person who extended the invitation usually foots the bill.

CHAOYANG

A Fun Ti Hometown Music Restaurant
(4, E11) $$
Uyghur
Stomach-swelling nosh, belly dancing and the exotic tunes of the A Fun Ti band – this Muslim minority knows how to have a good time. Size up a first-rate roasted lamb leg but beware of the jugs of beer – you may soon find yourself dancing on the long rows of wooden tables.
✉ 2288, 2 Houguai-bang Hutong ☎ 6527 2288 Ⓜ Chaoyangmen
🕙 10am-late

Ashanti Restaurant & Wine Bar (4, C13) $$
Spanish
Without bullfighting posters and straw donkeys, Ashanti has managed to tactfully capture the feel of a Spanish restaurant. *Escalibada* (grilled vegies), paella, and *crema catalana* (sweet flan) all go down nicely with sangria or decent bottles of Spanish and South African wine.
✉ cnr Gongren Tiyuchang Beilu & Chunxiu Lu ☎ 6416 6231 Ⓜ Dongsishitiao, then any bus east

🕙 11.30am-2.30pm & 6-11pm, wine bar 10.30pm-2am Ⓥ

Bifengtang (4, B12) $
Southern Chinese
Home-style Chinese cooking, right down to the gingham tablecloths and swinging garden benches. Try delicacies like sea cucumber, shark's fin or abalone from Hong Kong, Hunan, Guangdong and Hainan.
✉ 1 Xinzhong Jie, off Dongzhimen Wai Dajie ☎ 6415 2855
Ⓜ Dongzhimen
🕙 9.30am-9pm

Cherry Tree Café
(4, C12) $$$
European
If it seems a little nondescript, that's because it's exactly what you'd expect of a semi-formal European restaurant. Nothing too flashy, excellent service, and a calm atmosphere. It has a terrific breakfast buffet (6.30-10am; Y85) and an à la carte four-course meal for dinner (Y138).
✉ Asia Hotel, 8 Xinzhong Xijie ☎ 6500 7788

Ⓜ Dongsishitiao
🕙 6.30am-2pm & 6.30pm-midnight

Fu Jia Lou (4, C11) $
Traditional Beijing
Extremely popular with locals, this comfortable (and loud!) restaurant serves traditional Beijing fare for ridiculously good prices. If you don't speak Chinese, order from the pictures. Staff are keen to help and the service is great.
✉ 23 Dongsishitiao Lu ☎ 8403 7831
Ⓜ Dongsishitiao
🕙 11am-2pm & 5-10pm

Lemongrass
(4, C13) $$
Indian & Thai
The decor of this place is nothing special but the scrumptious curries, soups and tandoori get top ratings. There are a huge number of dishes to choose from, including some more unusual options like shark's fin (Y200) and fish baked in banana leaf. At Y28, the lunch buffet is a real bargain (but not as vegetarian-friendly as the menu). You can opt out of the fantastic service with takeaway.
✉ Chunxiu Lu ☎ 6416 9005
Ⓜ Dongsishitiao, then any bus east 🕙 11am-2pm & 5-10pm Ⓥ

Meizhou Dong Po
(4, B13) $$
Sichuanese
Sample some of China's

spiciest cuisine. The blistering-hot bean curd with chilli or dried chilli beef will have you screaming for water. This place is fairly popular – it's one of five around town – and its brightly painted interior lends a little charm.

✉ 7 Chunxiu Lu ☎ 6417 1566 Ⓜ Dongzhimen, then any bus east ☷ 11am-10.30pm

Metro Café (4, D13) $$$
Italian
Warm wood decor, the sound of clinking crystal, candlelight, soft jazz music and exceptional food – this is one of Beijing's classiest eateries. All pasta and sauces are made fresh on the premises and the wine list is extensive.

✉ 6 Gongren Tiyuchang Xilu ☎ 6551 6029 Ⓜ Dongsishitiao, then any bus east ☷ Mon-Fri 11.30am-2pm & 5.30pm-midnight, Sat-Sun 11.30am-midnight Ⓥ

Old Dock (4, C12) $$$
Chinese Seafood
Float in a very intimate, traditional Chinese riverboat while dining on an excellent selection of seafood. Boats on an indoor pond might sound tacky, but this is one of Beijing's most atmospheric and refined dining experiences.

✉ Asia Hotel, 8 Xinzhong Xijie, off Gongren Tiyuchang Beilu ☎ 6500 7788 Ⓜ Dongsishitiao ☷ 11.30am-2pm & 5.30-10pm

The warm and welcoming Metro Café

Outback Steakhouse (4, C13) $$$
Australian
Toss back a 'Wallaby Darned', wolf down your 'Bloomin' Onions' and dig into some baby back ribs, buffalo chicken wings or fresh seafood. This is a Western steakhouse through and through.

✉ Workers' Stadium (north entrance), Gongren Tiyuchang Beilu ☎ 6506 5166 Ⓜ Dongsishitiao, then any bus east ☷ 11am-2pm & 5-10.30pm ☷

Remember Café (4, B13) $
European/Chinese
The cryptic menu is a strange amalgamation of East meets West, or at least borscht meets 'spicy sheet jelly' and 'fish-smell eggplant'. Whatever it's meant to be, the food is pretty reasonable. The drinks menu is much steeper and much more impressive, with teas, coffees and cocktails, and the garden-swing chairs are very comfy.

✉ 10 Chunxiu Lu ☎ 6416 7681 Ⓜ Dongzhimen, then any bus east ☷ 8am-2am

Sunny Holiday Café (4, D13) $
Mediterranean
'Why go home when you can drop into the Sunny

Vegie Mantra
Following a strict vegetarian diet can be a tricky thing in Beijing. While you can order heaps of vegetables in Chinese restaurants, they're often cooked in animal fat. Vegetarian-by-choice is considered a bit of an oddity by most Chinese people and many don't understand that no meat means no chicken, lard or little bits of ground pork. Many travellers find that the easiest way to make themselves understood is to say that they're Buddhist *('Wo shi fojiao tu')*. For assurances of no meat, try **Green Tianshi Vegetarian Restaurant** (p71), or head out to the calming **Long Hwa Tree Organic Vegetarian Restaurant** (p78).

Holiday Café?' reads the card. This is a bit of an exaggeration; while it probably won't make you want to emigrate, its bright Mediterranean decor does brighten up a dreary day. Food from sunny holiday destinations includes kebabs, fajitas and pasta.
✉ 7 Gongren Tiyuchang Xilu ☎ 6551 3529 Ⓜ Dongsishitiao, then any bus east ⏱ 10am-2pm Ⓥ

Sunset Terrace
(4, C12) $$
Singaporean
On this outdoor 3rd-floor terrace, two chefs from Singapore prepare laksa noodles, satays and chicken rice. Help yourself at make-believe market stalls and

then dig in with some live music and a sunset backdrop.
✉ Swissotel, 2 Chao-yangmen Beidajie ☎ 6501 2288 Ⓜ Dongsishitiao ⏱ noon-10.30pm

Tasty-Taste (4, C13) $
Cakes
This sleek café has the most luxurious cakes in town (slice/whole cake Y13/130).
✉ cnr Gongren Tiyuchang Beilu & Gongren Tiyuchang Xilu ☎ 6551 1822 Ⓜ Dongsishitiao, then any bus east ⏱ 9am-11pm

Transit (4, C14) $$$
Modern Sichuanese
This place is elegant, right down to the indoor stream and traditional wooden

furniture. With soft music and impeccable service, enjoy innovative and gor-geously presented dishes.
✉ small alley opposite Workers' Stadium (north entrance), west of Xin Donglu ☎ 6417 6765 Ⓜ Dongsishitiao, then any bus east ⏱ noon-2pm & 5pm-midnight Ⓥ

Xinjiang Red Rose Restaurant (4, C14) $$
Uyghur
Not to be confused with Xin-jiang Restaurant on the main road, this traditional Muslim restaurant serves up huge portions of delicious food.
✉ alley off Gongren Tiyuchang Beilu ☎ 6415 5741 Ⓜ Dong-sishitiao, then any bus east ⏱ 11am-11pm

CHONGWEN & XUANWU

Fengzeyuan (6, B1) $$
Shandongese
A Beijing institution, this is where locals go to celebrate over Shandong specialities like sea cucum-ber with scallion or sautéed fish slices. Don't be surprised if diners next to you are busy toasting with round after round of snake wine.
✉ 83 Zhushikou Xidajie ☎ 6318 6688 ext 125 Ⓜ Qianmen, then bus 2 or 4 ⏱ 11am-2pm & 5-9pm

First Floor Restaurant
(4, K7) $
Beijing
This restaurant has the best *tang bao* (soup buns) around, as well as some

tasty scallion tofu and cold cucumber. It's not all that beautiful, but it's a favourite hangout for locals.
✉ 83 Qianmen Dajie ☎ 6303 0268

Ⓜ Qianmen ⏱ 9am-10.30pm

Goubuli (4, K6) $
Beijing
This famous Tianjin *baozi* outlet has started steaming

Waiter, Bill Please
Beijingers debate over the best, the worst and the crispiest around. One of the city's most famous recipes, delicious Peking duck has become an art form. The duck begins its journey to the table on a suburban farm, where it's fattened on grain and soybean paste. It then loses its feathers in exchange for a coating of molasses, is pumped up with air, filled with boiling water, dried and finally roasted over a fruitwood fire. It arrives at your table with crispy skin, boneless and decorated with shallots, plum sauce and crepes.

its buns in Beijing. It's canteen style, it's noisy and it's a great place to try big, plump dumplings stuffed with crab or pork. Shoppers pour in here all day long for refuelling. There's another branch west off Wangfujing Dajie.

✉ 31 Dazhalan Jie ☎ 6315 2389 M Qianmen ⏱ 9am-9pm

Liqun Roast Duck Restaurant (Liqun Kaoyadian) (4, K8) $$
Beijing
Buried away in a *hutong*, this well-known, pocket-sized eatery is full of activity. No medals for service but the duck is worth the wait. Reservations are required.

✉ 11 Beixiangfeng Hutong, off Zhengyi Lu ☎ 6702 5681 M Qianmen ⏱ 10am-10pm

Mian ai Mian (4, J6) $
Japanese
Huge bowls of steaming noodle soup, sushi and Japanese dumplings arrive at your table in minutes. The window seats are a great place to watch the buzzing street life around Qianmen.

✉ cnr Qianmen Xidajie & Qianmen Dajie ☎ 6303 5816 M Qianmen ⏱ 7.30am-9.30pm

Old Beijing Zhajiang Noodle King (6, C4) $
Beijing
This restaurant is a must. It's loud and busy and the perfect place to experience Chinese dining at its liveliest. Waiters arrive at your table with a large tray, and

with a fancy juggle that sends food flying through the air, they assemble your fresh noodles on the spot. The service is fantastic and the food even better.

✉ 29 Chongwai Jie, off Tiantan Lu ☎ 6705 6705 M Chongwenmen, then bus 43 or 60 ⏱ 11am-3pm & 5pm-midnight V

Qianmen Quanjude Roast Duck Restaurant (4, K7) $$$
Beijing
Despite the marketing devices and duck props, this has been one of the city's best roast-duck outlets since 1864. Two other branches are nearby.

✉ 32 Qianmen Dajie ☎ 6511 2418 M Qianmen ⏱ 11am-1.30pm & 4.45-8pm

Tianhai Canting (4, K6) $
Traditional Beijing
With a New Orleans meets

Chefs at work at Quanjude Roast Duck Restaurant

China look, this bistro serves sausage, duck, hotpot and lamb stew. The atmosphere is fantastic, with a gramophone in the corner, jars of snakes on the counter and black-and-white photos of old Beijing on the walls.

✉ 37 Dazhalan Jie ☎ 6304 4065 M Qianmen ⏱ 9am-midnight

It's all on show at Old Beijing Zhajiang Noodle King

DONGCHENG

Be There or Be Square
(4, H9) $
Cantonese
So it's not the coolest name and not exactly the classiest location, but it does have a pretty hip interior and it definitely does the business on Canto favourites like *cha siu* (barbecue pork), *siu mai* (prawn dumplings) and *chun kuen* (spring rolls). Give the spaghetti Bolognaise and other Western dishes a miss.
✉ BB71, Oriental Plaza, 1 Dongchang'an Jie
☎ 8518 6518 Ⓜ Wang-fujing ⏰ 24hrs

The Courtyard
(4, G7) $$$$
Fusion
Continental food with an Asian touch is served beneath a solarium

overlooking the moat of the Forbidden City. This chic restaurant serves some of Beijing's finest food, such as cashew-crusted lamb chops infused with spices from China's Muslim northwest. And views don't get much better than this.
✉ 95 Donghuamen Dajie ☎ 6526 8883
Ⓜ Tiananmen Dong
⏰ 6-9.30pm

Di Tangongyuan
(3, D11) $
Beijing
It's a bubbling frenzy inside, but this extremely popular restaurant serves up authentic local food. Fancy a bit of tofu paste, fried pickled fish or purple porridge? Rickshaws are waiting at the east gate of Ditan Park to whisk you to

the restaurant's front door.
✉ A1 Ditan Dongmen Wai ☎ 6427 3356
Ⓜ Yonghegong
⏰ 11am-2pm & 6-9pm

Donghua Yeshi Night Market (4, G8) $
Beijing, Hui & Uyghur
Grasshoppers, quail eggs and chicken hearts might not keep you coming back for more, but they will give you something to write home about. You can also find corn on the cob, strawberry kebabs, and fried potatoes for the less adventurous.
✉ Donganmen Dajie
Ⓜ Wangfujing, then bus 101 ⏰ 5.30-10.30pm

Fangshan Restaurant
(4, E5) $$$$
Traditional Beijing
Dine on imperial cuisine while overlooking the lake at Beihai Park. The gold decor in this restaurant is almost as elaborate as the food. Recipes are based on emperors' favourites such as deer tendon, peppery inkfish-egg soup and abalone. Reservations are a must.
✉ Jade Islet, Beihai Park (east gate) ☎ 6401 1889 Ⓜ Fuchengmen, then bus 101 ⏰ 11am-1.30pm & 5-8pm

Gonin Byakusho
(4, H8) $$$
Japanese
This is a quiet and simply decorated restaurant that specialises in *nimono* (boiled) and *yakimono*

Kebabs galore at Donghua Yeshi Night Market

(baked or roasted) Japanese dishes, as well as ornately presented sushi, tempura and sashimi.
✉ Basement, Beijing Hotel, 33 Dongchang'an Jie ☎ 6513 7766 ext 666 Ⓜ Wangfujing ⏱ 11.30am-2pm & 5.30-9.30pm

Green Tianshi Vegetarian Restaurant (4, F9) $$
Vegetarian
The atmosphere is peaceful and the decor is your typical Indian-restaurant affair. Bona fide vegetarians might have a hard time stomaching the make-believe meat but it's beautifully presented and you can be assured that nobody snuck even a pinch of animal product into your dish. Go on, try the lobster.
✉ 57 Dengshikou Jie ☎ 6524 2476 Ⓜ Wangfujing, then bus 101 ⏱ 10am-10pm Ⓥ

Kaorouji Restaurant (4, B6) $$
Muslim
Unfortunately, whoever painted the elaborate

Li Family Restaurant

Picky Eater
Royal dining was hefty work. Twice a day, Empress Dowager Cixi was presented with well over 100 dishes prepared by an army of 450 kitchen workers. Before being served, everything was taste-tested by a well-fed eunuch. As a final precaution, a strip of silver was placed into each dish, with discolouration signifying poison. In all that culinary chaos, it must have been difficult for the Empress to find the two or three dishes that she'd actually eat.

exterior never made it inside; the interior of this restaurant couldn't be more drab. But if you need to fill your belly, the tasty coriander roast mutton or the hot and sour soup should do the trick.
✉ 14 Qianhai Dongyan ☎ 6404 2554 Ⓜ Tiananmen Xi, then bus 5 ⏱ 11am-2pm & 5-10pm

Lai Jin Yu Xuan Restaurant (4, H6) $$
Traditional Chinese
In the west of Zhongshan Park, this traditional restaurant serves Ming and Qing dishes as described in the novel *Dream of the Red Mansion*, including a number of fish dishes. It looks as if it may have seen better days – not surprising considering it's been here since 1915.
✉ Zhongshan Park (west side) ☎ 6605 3507 Ⓜ Tiananmen Xi ⏱ 11am-4pm

Li Family Restaurant (Li Jia Cai) (4, B5) $$$$
Beijing
Step into the unpretentious home of the Li's, where Mrs Li creates masterpieces. Gastronomists take note: she can only squeeze three

or four tables into her front room, dining is by reservation only and in summer she can be booked up for weeks in advance.
✉ 11 Yangfang Hutong ☎ 6618 0107 🚌 58 ⏱ 6-8pm

Liujia Guo (4, G8) $$
Hunanese
This restaurant serves toned-down Hunan cuisine – only one handful of chillies instead of two. The grilled beef and braised pork come highly recommended. Vegetarians can tuck into the mock mutton or 'peasant family' style eggplant.
✉ 19 Nanheyan Dajie ☎ 6524 1487 Ⓜ Tiananmen Dong ⏱ 9am-noon Ⓥ

Mao's Family Restaurant (4, A9) $
Hunanese
Set in a sea of kitsch Mao memorabilia, this medium-spicy cuisine comes from Mao's hometown. Try the red-cooked pork, smoked fish fried with onions, or deep-fried pumpkin bread.
✉ 30 Yonghegong Dajie ☎ 8208 2609 Ⓜ Yonghegong ⏱ 11am-2pm & 5-10pm

Feeling peckish? Head to Wangfujing Snack Street

Red Capital Club
(4, D10) $$$
Beijing
Dine in a meticulously res-
tored Qing-styled courtyard
restaurant amongst 1950s
Politburo-meeting props.
The verbose menu lists each
dish with an accompanying
myth, but it's well worth the
work as the food is rated
Beijing's best and the
atmosphere is unique.
Reservations are required.
✉ 66 Dongsi Liutiao
☎ 6402 7150, 8401
8886 nights & weekends
Ⓜ Dongsishitiao,
then bus 115 or 118
◷ Mon-Sat 6-10pm

Scholtzsky's Deli (4, H9) $
American
The giant sandwiches on
freshly baked sourdough,
rye or wheat bread and the
home-made pizzas are all
good options.
✉ AA52, Oriental Plaza,
1 Dongchang'an Jie
☎ 8518 6810
Ⓜ Wangfujing
◷ 8am-9.30pm Ⓥ

Sichuan Fandian
(4, B5) $$$
Sichuanese
This place is famous among

locals and Chinese tourists
as the city's oldest Sichuanese restaurant. The fiery
food is very authentic;
try the duck that's been
marinated in wine for
24hrs, covered in tea leaves
and cooked over a charcoal
fire.
✉ 14 Liuyin Jie ☎ 6615
6924 🚌 5, 58, 118
◷ 11am-2pm & 5-9pm

Tony Roma's (4, H9) $$$
American
'Famous for ribs', Tony also
grills up chicken, shrimp
and burgers. The Family
Feast Platter will feed four
for Y280 and there are
crayons and colouring
placemats to keep the kids
busy while they wait for
their food.
✉ A305, Oriental Plaza,
1 Dongchang'an Jie
☎ 8518 6432
Ⓜ Wangfujing
◷ 11am-11pm ♿

Wangfujing Snack
Street (4, H8) $
Snacks
This pedestrianised street is
a jumble of atmosphere
and flavour. Stalls are
bursting with food from all
over China, including flat

bread, oodles of noodles
and pancakes. It's elbow to
elbow and definitely worth
a look.
✉ Wangfujing Jie
Ⓜ Wangfujing
◷ 11am-8pm

Yuanfu Kaiten Sushi
(4, H9) $
Japanese
Choose your sushi off the
conveyor belt in this Japanese diner. Or you can opt to
slurp noodles in the booths.
✉ AA73A, Oriental
Plaza, 1 Dongchang'an Jie
☎ 8518 6817
Ⓜ Wangfujing
◷ 10.30am-10pm

Yushan Restaurant
(4, C6) $$$
Traditional Beijing
The decor is fairly grim, but
how often do you get to try
scorpions? Dishes are made
according to recipes from
the Qing royal kitchen. It's a
popular place for wedding
banquets and parties, so
reservations are a must.
✉ Beihai Park
☎ 6401 5855 🚌 115,
118 ◷ 10.30am- 2pm &
4-7.30pm

JIANGUOMENWAI EMBASSY AREA

Ah Yat Abalone Restaurant
(4, H15) $$$$
Cantonese
This large, banquet-style restaurant is somewhat lacking in atmosphere. It's favoured by Cantonese visitors and has some of the freshest abalone in town.
✉ 1a Jianguomen Wai Dajie ☎ 6508 9613 Ⓜ Guo Mao ⏱ 10am-10.30pm

Bleu Marine (4, G14) $$
French
It's well located, pleasantly decorated and the food is rich and fairly good, even if the accompanying rice isn't very French. There's a new menu daily, with dishes like onion soup and veal stew.
✉ 5 Guanghua Xilu ☎ 6500 6704 Ⓜ Yong An Li ⏱ 11.30am-10.30pm

Danieli's (4, H12) $$$
Italian
This small, grandiose restaurant serves up fresh gourmet pasta and has a fairly good wine list.
✉ 2nd fl, St Regis Hotel, 21 Jianguomen Wai Dajie ☎ 6460 6688 ext 2440 Ⓜ Jianguomen ⏱ 11am-2pm & 6-10pm

The Elephant
(4, F13) $
Russian
Fill up on borscht, herring and stroganoff to the beat of Russian polkas. The decor, the huge menu, the well-stocked bar and the expat clientele are all very authentic.
✉ 17 Ritan Beilu ☎ 8561 4013 Ⓜ Jianguomen, then bus 29 ⏱ 11am-3am

Henry J Bean's
(4, H15) $$
American
Why do so many Westerners find themselves holed up at Henry's? There must be something addictive in the French onion soup or succulent burgers. Or maybe it's just because you can buy beer by the pint. Show up after 9pm for the nightly live music gig.
✉ L129, West Wing, China World Trade Centre, 1 Jianguomen Wai Dajie ☎ 6505 2266 ext 6569 Ⓜ Guo Mao ⏱ 11am-2am

Justine's (4, H14) $$$$
French
C'est fantastique! This French cuisine is the real thing – goose liver, fresh oysters, caviar, cheeses and champagne. It's well worth the francs.
✉ Jianguo Hotel Beijing, Jianguomen Wai Dajie ☎ 6500 2233 Ⓜ Yong An Li ⏱ 6.30-9.30am, noon-2.30pm & 6-10.30pm

Dinner at the Big Table

Other than a few American-style family restaurants, Chinese eateries don't appear to 'specialise' in being kid-friendly. This doesn't mean that you should leave your little ones at home – in fact, quite the opposite. In a traditionally family-oriented culture, where aunts mind nephews and nieces and parents look after their grannies, bringing kids to the dinner table is the norm. Waitresses will cuddle them and other diners will ooh and aah. Highchairs are a rarity but communal dishes that are part of Chinese dining make it easy to create tyke-sized portions, and if the kids become rambunctious and spill their food, they'll fit right in.

Makye Ame (4, H13) $
Tibetan
Slurp back some yak-butter tea and soak in the atmosphere while prayer flags flap in the window. The menu is excellent and the cushions are comfy.
✉ 2nd fl, 11 Xiushui Nanjie ☎ 6507 9966
Ⓜ Jianguomen
🕓 11am-10.30pm

Phrik Thai (4, G12) $$
Thai
This cosy, relaxed restaurant has lots of tasty Thai barbeque, curries and soups, and very friendly staff.
✉ The Gateway, 10 Yabao Lu (running south off main Yabao Lu)
☎ 8561 5236
Ⓜ Jianguomen, then any bus north
🕓 11.30am-2pm & 5.30-10.30pm

Sammie's (4, H14) $
Café
This is a great place for a snack after shopping next door at the Silk Market. It has great sandwich combos, mellow pop music and excellent fruit smoothies. As the slogan says, it's 'Where East Eats West'.
✉ cnr Jianguomen Wai Dajie & Sanlitun Nanjie

Enjoy the yak meat at Makye Ame

☎ 6506 8838
Ⓜ Yong An Li 🕓 9am-midnight Ⓥ

Taj Pavilion (4, H15) $$$
Indian
Mild and not-so-mild curries, creamy textures and exotic flavourings will satisfy your stomach's cravings for a taste of India.
✉ L1, West Wing, China World Trade Centre, 1 Jianguomen Wai Dajie
☎ 6505 2288 ext 8116
Ⓜ Guo Mao
🕓 11.30am-2.30pm & 6-10.30pm Ⓥ

Xiao Wang's Home Restaurant (4, G14) $$
Chinese
Home-style cuisine is fiery at Xiao's place. Try the deservedly famous Xinjiang-style chicken wings or pepper salt spareribs. Dine in the conservatory or in rooms along the corridor.
✉ 2 Guanghua Dongli
☎ 6581 3255 Ⓜ Yong An Li 🕓 11am-2pm & 5-10pm

Xiheyaju Restaurant (4, F13) $$
Sichuanese
Enjoy excellently prepared dishes in the leafy, bright conservatory. This place is a longstanding favourite of expats and locals.
✉ Ritan Park ☎ 8561 7643 Ⓜ Jianguomen, then bus 29 🕓 11am-2pm & 5-10pm

Magnifique! The table setting at Justine's

SANLITUN EMBASSY AREA

1001 Nights (4, C15) $
Middle Eastern
If you've got a craving for hummus, Armenian salads or very sweet sweets, sit yourself down beneath the Arabian arches of 1001 Nights.
✉ Gongren Tiyuchang Beilu, opp Zhaolong Hotel ☎ 6532 4050 Ⓜ Dong-shitiao, then bus 113 🕑 11am-2am Ⓥ

Athena Greek Restaurant (4, B14) $$
Greek
Whitewashed walls, splashes of blue, and Greek music will have you believing you're on an island in the Mediterranean. The food is authentic – try the stuffed vine leaves or Greek salad. There's a 20% discount for group reservations and you can have food delivered to your hotel door.
✉ 1 Xiwu Jie ☎ 6464 6036 Ⓜ Dongzhimen 🕑 11am-2pm & 6-10pm

Bella (4, C14) $
Café
Escape from the bustling market next door for fresh bagels and subs and 'real' coffee from the espresso machine. You can also indulge in cheesecake or chocolate and banana mousse.
✉ Sanlitun Yashou Clothing Market, Gongren Tiyuchang Beilu ☎ 6417 3449 Ⓜ Dongsishitiao, then bus 113 🕑 8.30am-8pm Ⓥ

Berena's Bistro (4, D14) $$
Chinese
This cosy Chinese restaurant is a time-honoured favourite. The food leans towards Sichuan and can be heavy on the chilli. Try the hot and sour soup, the chicken in spicy sauce or the beef platter with black pepper. There's a play area for the kids while you taste your way through the bar's many imported beers.
✉ 6 Gongrentiyuguan Donglu ☎ 6592 2628 Ⓜ Dongsishitiao, then any bus east 🕑 6-10pm ♿ Ⓥ

Da Cheng Yong He (4, C14) $
Chinese Fast Food
Conveniently located near Sanlitun Bar Street, you can order Chinese-style brekky from an English menu any time of the day. For a fast-food outlet, it's remarkably comfortable.
✉ Xin Donglu Ⓜ Dongsishitiao, then any bus east 🕑 24hrs

Frank's Place (4, D14) $$
American Pub Grub
Easily recognisable as an American bar, you can get classic American burgers, spuds, buffalo wings, and steak and Guinness pie. There's also an all-day breakfast menu, beer on tap, pool tables and sports on the big screen. This is very much an expat hangout.
✉ Gongrentiyuguan Donglu ☎ 6507 2617 Ⓜ Dongsishitiao, then any bus east 🕑 2pm-midnight

Geng Wu Mess (4, C14) $
Beijing
This hole-in-the-wall eatery serves classic Beijing fare such as cornbread stuffed with pork, and spinach and meatballs. With wooden benches and traditional paintings on the walls, it's simple but cosy and very atmospheric. Look for the giant golden coin hanging outside.
✉ 12 Xin Donglu ☎ 6416 5186 Ⓜ Dongsishitiao, then any bus east 🕑 6-10pm

Golden Elephant (4, C14) $$
Thai & Indian
Long established and deservedly popular, the raved-about food is elegantly presented. Try the branch on Nonzhanguan Nanlu, which specialises in Thai and Indian barbecue.
✉ west off Sanlitun Lu ☎ 6417 2139 Ⓜ Dongsishitiao, then bus 113 🕑 6-10.30pm Ⓥ

Green Tea House (4, B14) $$$$
Chinese
With a blend of traditional and modern design, this place is a stunner and is totally soothing. The innovative menu offers sumptuous dishes like 'Little Clouds of Dumpling in Green Tea Consume' and 'Roasted Rabbit on a Bed of Rose-Jasmine Creamy

Mediterraneo's offerings

Mushrooms'. There's also an extensive tea menu – you can chill out with a bottomless cup for hours.
✉ 53 Tayuancun Xilujie
☎ 6468 5903
M Dongzhimen
⏱ 11am-midnight

Kebab Kafe (4, C14) $$
European
This place has a European menu, sports on the TV and not a great deal of atmosphere. Nevertheless, it's remained a favourite for many foreigners, who come here for the Swiss fondue, the fish and the pasta.
✉ 46 Sanlitun Lu

☎ 6415 5812 M Dongsishitiao, then bus 113 ⏱ noon-2pm & 6-10pm

Kejia Yuan (4, D15) $
Southern Chinese
This restaurant's wooden beams and enclosed booths give it a rural feel. Chefs cook with lilies and lotuses, Guangzhou style.
✉ 2 Dongsanhuan Beilu
☎ 6582 5010
M Dongsishitiao, then bus 113 ⏱ 11am-1.30pm & 6-10pm

Matsuko (4, D15) $$
Japanese
With fresh ingredients flown in daily, this modern restaurant is a favourite with Japanese expats.
✉ 22 Dongsanhuan Beilu ☎ 6582 5208
M Dongsishitiao, then bus 113 ⏱ 11.30am-2pm & 5-10.30pm

Mediterraneo (4, B15) $$
Mediterranean
This place has a fantastic menu of delicious pastas, tapas, risottos, salads and fish and meat off the grill. Its candlelit patio and lively

---

atmosphere make it a fantastic place to dine.
✉ 8 Sanlitun Lu
☎ 6415 3691
M Dongsishitiao, then bus 113 ⏱ 11am-2pm & 6-10pm V

No 44 (4, C15) $
Café
Window seats and sidewalk tables make this small, relaxed café a great place to people-watch along Sanlitun Lu. Grab a cappuccino, fruit smoothie or a pastry and enjoy the chill-out music.
✉ 44 Sanlitun Lu
M Dongsishitiao, then bus 113 ⏱ 11am-10pm

Serve the People (4, C15) $$
Thai
Ignore the uninspired name and prepare for Beijing's most fashionable Thai restaurant. Its warm decor, *tom yam* (spicy, lemongrass-flavoured soup) and Thai barbecue won't disappoint.
✉ 3 Sanlitun Xiwujie
☎ 8454 4580
M Dongsishitiao, then bus 113 ⏱ 10.30am-10.30pm V

Tuanjiehu Roast Duck Restaurant (4, D15) $$
Beijing
Beneath its recently spruced-up decor, this is still the same old favourite duckery, serving lean birds and mean sugared duck skin (an imperial inclination).
✉ 3 Tuanjiehu Beikou, off Dongsanhuan Beilu
☎ 6582 2892 M Guo Mao, then bus 113 ⏱ 11am-2pm & 5-9.30pm

Views to Dine For
While Beijing has a lot of restaurants high in the sky, their food isn't always as tops as their views. It's well worth reserving for those that do satisfy. For an excellent fusion meal overlooking the moat, edged with the golden splendour of the Forbidden City, book at **The Courtyard** (p70). In summer the **Sunset Terrace** (p68) serves South-Asian cuisine outdoors before a brilliant sinking sun. **Belle Vue** (p77) will spin you around at dizzying heights for 360-degree views of northern Beijing as you chomp on your peppercorn steak.

SANLITUN NORTH

Belle Vue (4, A15) $$$
European
It's a little bit run down, but as you cut into your T-bone steak or veal, you can enjoy some tops views from this revolving restaurant.
✉ Kunlin Hotel, 2 Xinyuan Nanlu
☎ 6590 3388 ext 5507
🚌 300, 302, 403
🕙 5.30-11.30pm

Genji (3, D13) $$$$
Japanese
Dine in a private tatami room or at the teppanyaki grills in this low-key, traditional Japanese restaurant. For lunch you can feast on unlimited sushi with free-flowing Sapporo for Y258.
✉ 2nd fl, Hilton Hotel, 1 Dongfang Lu ☎ 6466 2288 🚌 302, 403
🕙 11.30am-2pm & 6-10pm

Louisiana (3, D13) $$$$
American
Not to be outshone by a famous wine list, the kitchen delivers prime beef flown in chilled from the US. There is also excellent Cajun and Creole cuisine and fantastic seafood.
✉ 2nd fl, Hilton Hotel, 1 Dongfang Lu, off Beisanhuan Donglu ☎ 6466 2288 ext 7420 🚌 302, 403 🕙 11.30am-2pm & 6-10pm

Paulaner Brauhaus (3, D13) $$$
German
Sauerkraut, sausage and beer by the barrel – this is a meat and beer-lover's

Meal Deals
If you're looking to impress your clients (or clients-to-be) Chinese-style, take them to the classy and relatively quiet **Xiheyaju Restaurant** (p74). For something a bit more contemporary, book the private room at **Transit** (p68), or for a tête-à-tête, the calm **Green Tea House** (p75) will keep the client cool-headed. If cutlery makes you more confident, try the **Metro Café** (p67).

fantasy. The brewery pumps out pints to be soaked up by heavy breads and liverwurst. There's live oom-pa-pa music and weekend barbecues in the summer.
✉ Youyi Lufthansa Centre, Liangmaqiao Lu ☎ 6465 3388 ext 5732 Ⓜ Guo Mao, then bus 207 🕙 11am-1am

Red Basil (3, D13) $$$
Thai
High ceilings and simple but lovely adornments make this a classy place to dine on fiery food.
✉ Beisanhuan Donglu ☎ 6460 2339 🚌 302, 403 🕙 11.30am-2pm & 5.30-10pm Ⓥ

Salsa Cabana (3, D13) $$
Latin American
Bright and chrome-encrusted, this place tries really hard for atmosphere but doesn't quite hit the

mark. You can fill up on unlimited chilli con carne at lunch and take a salsa lesson on Thursday or Saturday evenings.
✉ Youyi Lufthansa Centre, 50 Liangmaqiao Lu ☎ 6465 3388 ext 5700 Ⓜ Guo Mao, then bus 207 🕙 Sun-Thurs 11.30am-2am, Fri-Sat 11.30am-3.30am

Sorobal (3, D13) $$
Korean
Excellent *banfan* (rice, egg, meat, vegies and hot pepper sauce) and *paigu* (roast spareribs) are served at this top-end, slightly stuffy restaurant.
✉ Youyi Lufthansa Centre, 50 Liangmaqiao Lu ☎ 6465 3388 Ⓜ Guo Mao, then bus 207 🕙 11.30am-2pm & 6-10pm

Sui Yuan (3, D13) $$$
Cantonese
Choose your fish, giant crab or lobster straight out of the aquarium. You can also try abalone, sea cucumber and shark's fin in this seafood nirvana. Enjoy one of Beijing's more extensive dim sum menus here.
✉ 2nd fl, Hilton Hotel, 1 Dongfang Lu, off Beisanhuan Donglu
☎ 6466 2288 ext 7416
🚌 302, 403
🕐 11.30am-2pm & 6-10pm, dim sum Mon-Fri 11.30am-2pm

Trattoria La Gondola (3, D13) $$
Italian
Devour thin-crusted pizza (Italiano style), cheese-covered pasta dishes and excellent breads. It's a little over-decorated but it's family friendly and the food is fairly authentic.
✉ Youyi Lufthansa Centre, 50 Liangmaqiao Lu ☎ 6465 3388 ext 5707 🚌 Guo Mao, then bus 207 🕐 11.30am-2pm & 5.30-11pm
♿ Ⓥ

XICHENG

Nengrenjo (4, E2) $$
Hotpot
Dip scrumptious lamb slices or skewered vegies into rich sesame sauce at Beijing's most renowned hotpot restaurant. Loyal patrons are wall to wall in winter so book ahead or come early.
✉ 5 Taipingqiao Dajie
☎ 6601 2560
Ⓜ Fuchengmen
🕐 10.30am-2am

Shaguoju (4, F3) $
Beijing
This place is famous for its clay-pot pork dishes and its tenacious hold on the Beijing palate.
✉ 60 Xisi Nandajie
☎ 6602 1126 Ⓜ Xidan, then any bus north
🕐 11am-10pm

Breakfast Hao?
Doujiang (soybean milk), *youtiao* (fried dough sticks) and *zongzi* (sticky rice wrapped in lotus leaves) — breakfast in Beijing is heavy, but it'll stick to your ribs until lunch. To try some traditional brekky, visit roadside vendors or **Da Cheng Yong He** (p75).

WORTH THE TREK

Away (3, D6) $
Café
Leaf through a magazine, sip coffee and cocktails or slurp noodles in this small, book-lined, artsy café. Art-house films are shown each Tuesday and local scholars occasionally give talks.
✉ Wegongcun Lu
☎ 6845 1147
🚌 double-decker No 4
🕐 2pm-2am

Jiuhuashan Roast Duck Restaurant (3, F6) $$$
Beijing
Atmosphere is nowhere to be seen and it's a trek to get here, but duck connoisseurs *insist* this is the way duck is meant to taste.
✉ Ziyu Hotel, 55 Zengguang Lu ☎ 6848 3481 Ⓜ Fuchengmen or Chegongzhuang (then 4km by taxi) 🕐 11am-2pm & 5-9pm

Long Hwa Tree Organic Vegetarian Restaurant (3, C2) $
Vegetarian
Run by the Fan family, this place is filled with a unique peacefulness. The menu changes daily, with dishes like spicy Indian curry, delicious Taiwanese rice noodles, and thick vegie sandwiches. Food is laid-out buffet style — create your own portions and then pay 'according to your own good heart and mind'. Drop your money into the large ceramic jar in the corner; these kind and trusting souls won't even ask.
✉ 3 Mai Mai Jie (east of Fragrant Hills Park east gate) 🚌 333 from Summer Palace, 360 from Beijing Zoo, 318 from Pingguoyuan station
🕐 9am-3pm Ⓥ

Entertainment

A new kind of electricity is pouring through the streets of Beijing and riding on its wave is a new breed of Beijingers – out on the town and ready to have a good time. Whether you're interested in watching jugglers, listening to live jazz, sipping a martini or swiggin' a beer, chances are you'll be impressed with what Beijing has to offer. The shackles of authority have been loosened and new bars and clubs are cropping up all over town, run by a young, more worldly generation. These venues have got plenty of atmosphere, play cutting-edge music and are quickly over-taking the stale karaoke-pumping, *baijiu*-slinging drinking holes of the past. The capital also hosts scores of nightly performances of Chinese opera and acrobatics, where you can immerse yourself in the more traditional forms of entertainment.

Theatre is, perhaps, the only art that still appears rather stifled. The Cultural Revolution didn't exactly help it along and stage drama has never faired well against the competition from opera and DVD. These days, more plays do get a curtain call and there are a growing number of theatres where you can check out local thespians.

Entrance into the majority of clubs and bars is free or, at most, reasonably priced, with drinks costing around Y30. Opera and acrobatic performances have long been on the tourist route and can be a little bit

> **Top Spots**
>
> If you fancy a drink, a boogie and a bit of live music, **Sanlitun** is where it's at. The main drag (nicknamed Sanlitun Bar Street) appears to be breeding so many bars that they're overflowing into the streets and alleys around it. The crowd here is a mixed bag of tourists, locals and expats, and the venues range from chilled to booming. East of here, the area around **Chaoyang Amusement Park** is a pocket of sleazy pick-up joints. The giant exception to this is the World of Suzie Wong, Beijing's best club. On the west bank of **Qianhai Lake** is a growing number of bars and late-night cafés where lots of locals and a few tourists drink. Theatres and cinemas are dotted around town.

Catching up at the Buddha Café

pricier. For all tickets, book directly with the venue, or for theatre and concerts try the toll-free hotline ☎ 800 8100 443.

Information

There's a range of English-language listings and entertainment magazines that you can pick up in hotel lobbies or Western supermarkets. The most comprehensive is *that's Beijing*, a monthly magazine with independent, opinionated listings. *BJ (Beijing Journal)*, *Beijing This Month* and *Beijing Focus* are all monthly and all contain OK listings. *Metrozine* is a fortnightly, bilingual publication focusing on Beijing's art scene.

SPECIAL EVENTS

late January/early February *Chinese New Year* – the biggest festival of the year, celebrated with three days of temple fairs (visit Lama Temple, Ditan Park and White Cloud Temple) and family bonding
Lantern Festival – 15 days after Chinese New Year, this colourful festival parades through the evening streets in search of airborne spirits

March *International Women's Day* – 8 March; a public holiday with little fanfare
Birthday of Guanyin, Goddess of Mercy – a great time to visit Buddhist and Taoist temples

April *Tomb Sweeping Day* – 5 April; a day for worshipping ancestors by cleaning gravesites and burning ghost money

late April/early May *Tianhou Festival* – Taoists celebrate the birth of the Goddess of the Sea and Protector of Fishermen

May *International Labour Day* – 1 May; the entire city, particularly Tiananmen Square, is blanketed in flowers

June *Children's Day* – 1 June; kites blot out the sky

July *Anniversary of the Founding of the Chinese Communist Party* – 1 July; official flag waving in Tiananmen Square

August *Anniversary of the Founding of the People's Liberation Army* – 1 August; more official flag waving in Tiananmen Square
Ghost Month – when ghosts from hell walk the earth; it's considered a bad time to swim, travel, marry or move house

September *Mid-Autumn Festival* – also known as Moon Festival; families get together and chow down on moon cakes

October *National Day* – 1 October; marching bands come rolling out
Confucius' Birthday – aptly celebrated at Confucius Temple

November *International Jazz Festival* – groove to the rhythms of jazz bands from around the globe

BARS & LOUNGES

Artefacts Café & Bar
(3, E13) The Chinese-Cuban fusion makes for a cool, spacious and relaxed bar. Lounge in traditional wooden chairs, snacking on olives and listening to R&B tunes.
✉ 5 Nongzhanguan Nanlu ☎ 6592 7141 Ⓜ Dongsishitiao, then bus 115 ⏱ 2pm-late

Bridge Bar (4, B6)
The rooftop terrace has views over Silver Ingot Bridge and the warm, wooden interior is a pleasant place to enjoy a tea, coffee or something a little stronger.
✉ Qianhai Dongyan (first bldg east of bridge) Ⓜ Gulou Dajie, then taxi; or Tiananmen Xi, then bus 5 ⏱ 2pm-late

Buddha Café (4, C6)
With black-and-white photos of Beijing's *hutongs*, wooden benches and a great drinks menu, this is a comfortable place to relax. In summer its lakeside tables are deservedly popular. There's another smaller branch a few doors down.
✉ 2 Yinding Qiao ☎ 6617 9488 🚌 118 ⏱ 2pm-2am

Charlie's Bar (4, H14)
This somewhat yesteryear but still august bar has velvety walls and a view across a small stream. It's a favourite of nearby embassy staff.
✉ Jianguo Hotel, 5 Jianguomen Wai Dajie ☎ 6500 2233 Ⓜ Yong An Li ⏱ 11.30am-late

The Courtyard (4, G7)
Upstairs from the restaurant is a tiny cigar room where you can sip port in a leather chair and take in the perfectly framed view of the Forbidden City's east gate and surrounding moat.
✉ 95 Donghuamen Dajie ☎ 6526 8883 Ⓜ Tiananmen Dong ⏱ 6-9.30pm

The Den (4, C14)
A giant TV screen beams down at you from the corner of this dark bar. This place has seen better days but remains popular and is packed out on Saturday nights.
✉ 4 Gongti Donglu ☎ 6592 6290 Ⓜ Dongsishitiao, then bus 113 ⏱ 9am-3am

Havana Café (4, C13)
With salsa dancing, patio tables and lots of marketing around town, this place is extremely popular with foreigners.
✉ Workers' Stadium (north entrance) ☎ 6586 6166 Ⓜ Dongsishitiao, then any bus east ⏱ 6pm-late

Hidden Tree (4, D14)
Sitting on this leafy, intimate patio, you'd never guess you were next to a booming bar street. Inside it's snug and the cellar is full of Belgian brews.
✉ 12 Dongdaqiaoxie Jie (South Sanlitun Bar Street) ☎ 6509 3642 Ⓜ Dongsishitiao, then bus 113 ⏱ 11am-4am

Hou Hai Café & Bar
(4, B6) This low-key,

beautifully decorated café and bar has large rattan chairs from which you can enjoy a view of cyclists, vendors, sightseers and locals wandering past Houhai Lake. It serves teas, coffees, beers and liqueurs.

✉ 20 Houhai Nanyan
☎ 6613 6209
Ⓜ Gulou Dajie, then taxi; or Tiananmen Xi, then bus 5
☽ noon-2am

Jasmine Garden (4, C14)
Relaxing on comfy couches inside a simply decorated room, the mainly Chinese clientele sip incredibly strong cocktails to the vibes of house and trance music.

✉ Dongdaqiaoxie Jie (South Sanlitun Bar Street) Ⓜ Dongsishitiao, then bus 113
☽ 2pm-late

Neon nights in Sanlitun

Rocket Fuel

You've probably already caught a whiff of it. If you've tried it – and remember trying it – you're almost certainly blessed with the liver of an ox. *Baijiu* (white spirit) is the Chinese answer to Russian vodka or Mexican tequila. It's sweet and clear and goes down like rocket fuel. Beijing men (and, increasingly, women) drink it by the bucketful with meals, to celebrate or just to pass the time. For less than Y10, *baijiu* will make your world fuzzy, play havoc with your motor skills and cause you to forget your own name. Erguotou is the 'connoisseurs' brand; it comes in handy 5L plastic drums.

La Rive Gauche (4, C6)
A swanky but quiet wine bar that has huge leather couches, local art on the walls, a great wine list and a collection of fishbowls, flowers and potted plants.

✉ 11 Qianhai Beiyan
☎ 6612 9300
Ⓜ Gulou Dajie, then taxi; or Tiananmen Xi, then bus 5 ☽ 2pm-2am

Neo Lounge (4, C14)
Very chic, this is where Beijing's young, sophisticated crowd come to lounge. There's a good wine list, champers and imported beer, and the music includes ambient, house and chill-out, with occasional live jazz.

✉ 99 Xingfuyicun Lu
☎ 6316 1077
Ⓜ Dongsishitiao, then bus 113 ☽ 6pm-2am

No Name Bar (4, B6)
This bar offers an escape into a relaxed subtropical zone. Peer through the jungle of greenery and wind

chimes to Qianhai Lake.

✉ 3 Qianhai Dongyan
☎ 6401 8541
Ⓜ Gulou Dajie, then taxi; or Tiananmen Xi, then bus 5
☽ 2pm-late

Passby Bar (4, C7)
Catering to tumbleweed travellers, this courtyard bar has polished beams, a mezzanine and a useful library of travel books. The travel-oriented staff serve up piles of info on the capital.

✉ 108 Nanluogu Xiang
☎ 8403 8004
🖳 pass_by@sina.com
Ⓜ Dongsishitiao, then bus 115
☽ 11am-2.30am

Press Club (4, H12)
This intimate, wood-panelled bar has the posh air of a private, old boys' club.

✉ St Regis, 21 Jianguomen Wai Dajie
☎ 6460 6688
Ⓜ Jianguomen
☽ 2pm-late

PUBS

Black Jack Garden
(4, C14) With Harley-Davidson paintings, faux-wood panelling and beer on tap, this small hangout succeeds in creating a mid-West American bar atmosphere.
✉ small alley opp Workers' Stadium (north entrance) ☎ 6417 4628 Ⓜ Dongsishitiao, then any bus east ⏲ 5pm–2am

Downtown Café **(4, D14)**
With cheap food, beer and a dartboard, this quiet Western-style pub is a favourite weekday hideaway for expats.
✉ 7 Gongti Donglu ☎ 6507 3407 Ⓜ Dongsishitiao, then any bus east ⏲ noon–2am

Durty Nellie's **(4, D14)**
It seems every city has an Irish pub; Beijing's is rather cavernous but more authentic than most, with genuine Guinness and Kilkenny's, wobbly tables straight from Dublin, hits from the Corrs

and a regular band cranking out Eire ballads.
✉ 11a Dongdaqiaoxie Jie (South Sanlitun Bar Street) ☎ 6502 2808 Ⓜ Dongsishitiao, then any bus east ⏲ noon–1am

Frank's Place **(4, D14)**
Sports on the big screen, Carlsberg and Guinness on tap and pool tables at the back; Frank provides a recognisable 'slice of home' for North Americans. It's very popular with expats who come here after a hard round of golf. You can fill up on buffalo wings and burgers and breakfast is available round the clock.
✉ Gongti Donglu ☎ 6507 2617 Ⓜ Dongsishitiao, then any bus east ⏲ noon–1am

Huxley's **(4, D14)**
Lively, with no frills, this is the place to come to soak up some of the *baijiu* with pizza and then chase it with some beer. The crowd

Shoot pool at Frank's

is mostly young foreigners.
✉ 2nd alley west off Dongdaqiaoxie Jie (South Sanlitun Bar Street) ☎ 6500 1251 Ⓜ Dongsishitiao, then bus 113 ⏲ 6pm–late

Poachers **(4, C14)**
With pop music bouncing off the high ceilings, the young, friendly crowd in this popular pub is a great mix of foreigners and locals. The beer's on tap and wine is sold by the bottle.
✉ 43 Beisanlitun Lu ☎ 6417 2632 Ⓜ Dongsishitiao, then bus 113 ⏲ 5.30pm–late

Doing that Cha-Cha Thing

Calm and atmospheric, traditional Chinese teahouses are an alternative to Beijing's hopping bar and pub scene. Native to China and cultivated for the last 2000 years, *cha* (tea) is the fuel of the nation. Nonfermented tea is most commonly recognised as Chinese green tea. Black tea (English tea) is fully fermented and Wulong is somewhere in between. Scented tea contains fragrant flowers such as jasmine. Teahouses serve refined and often rare tea, accompanied by seeds and sweets. Allow your tea to steep for as long as it takes the leaves to sink to the bottom of the cup; when you're ready for more hot water, place the lid on the table. Savour a cup of China's finest in the private, bamboo rooms of the **Tea Garden** (4, C12; Poly Plaza, 14 Dongzhimen Nandajie; ☎ 6500 1188) or at the **Purple Vine Teahouse** (4, G6; 2 Nanchang Jie; ☎ 6606 6614) amid strains of classical music and wafts of incense.

CLUBS & DISCOS

Cross Club (4, C14)
When you tire of shaking your booty on the tiny dance floor, head upstairs to the comfortable, traditional Chinese lounge bar. Smoke a cigar, snack on dumplings and garlic bread, and shoot some pool.
✉ 1 Beisanlitun Jie
☎ 6415 8318
Ⓜ Dongsishitiao, then bus 113 ⏱ 8pm-late

Latinos (3, E14)
You can salsa and merengue to bands flown in from South America or just watch Beijingers boogie to Latin beats. Beware: the sleaze from neighbouring clubs already seems to be creeping into this newcomer. Call for dance class details.
✉ Chaoyang Amusement Park (south gate)

☎ 6507 9898
Ⓜ Dongsishitiao, then bus 113 ⏱ 11am-2am

The Loft (4, C15)
Looking a bit like LA in the '80s, this popular and comfortable club has an outdoor garden, art gallery and a dance floor for those moved by the jazz, techno and house music.
✉ 4 Gongren Tiyuchang Beilu (down alley next to Pacific Department Store)
☎ 6501 7501
Ⓜ Dongsishitiao, then bus 113 ⏱ 11am-2am

Nadine's (4, D14)
Funk, R&B and reggae explode from this coarse but friendly club. It's popular with American and African expats and is a good place to get funky.
✉ 11 Dongdaqiaoxie Jie

(South Sanlitun Bar Street)
Ⓜ Dongsishitiao, then bus 113 ⏱ 8pm-late

No 55 (4, C14)
This small place screams industrial minimalism and yet its comfy chairs, Latin jazz vibes and long cocktail menu make it a welcoming place for a drink and a dance.
✉ small alley opposite Workers' Stadium (north entrance) ☎ 6416 2063
Ⓜ Dongsishitiao, then any bus east ⏱ 8pm-late

Orange (4, C13)
This atmospheric, trendy club has soft lighting, couches and a dance floor where you can groove to R&B and hip-hop. It has visiting DJs from the far west and lots of drink specials.
✉ 2-10 Xingfu Yicun (alley across from Workers' Stadium, north entrance) ☎ 6415 7413
Ⓜ Dongsishitiao, then any bus east ⏱ 9pm-3am $ free-Y20

Public Space (4, C15)
This is Sanlitun's pacesetter and longest resident. It's managed to maintain its atmosphere and remains popular with the 'see-and-be-seen' crowd. DJs spin house music in the evenings.
✉ 50 Sanlitun Lu
☎ 6416 0759
Ⓜ Dongsishitiao, then bus 113 ⏱ 10am-2am

R&B (4, D14)
Come here for the friendly

crowds and the fantastic funk, soul and R&B music rather than the basic, student-like decor.

✉ **Xi 8 Bldg, Dongdaqiaoxie Jie (2nd alley west off South Sanlitun Bar Street)** ☎ 6502 5595 Ⓜ Dongsishitiao, then bus 113 ☾ 8pm-late

Vic's (4, C13)
This club has couches, a pool table and a sweaty dance floor. It draws diverse crowds; most nights the music is R&B, hip-hop and pop, but on Thursday night reggae rules. Ladies' night on Wednesday is a sordid affair.

✉ **Workers' Stadium (north entrance)** ☎ 6593 6215 Ⓜ Dongsishitiao, then any bus east ☾ 7pm-late $ Sun-Thurs free, Fri-Sat Y30

Vogue
Beijing's premier dance club is busy moving. It will soon reopen its doors so that DJs and live music can once again draw feverish clubbers to its heaving dance floor. To find out

DJ-ing the night away in a Beijing club

where and when, check with Neo Lounge (p82).

The World of Suzie Wong (3, E14)
A 1930s Shanghai opium den has collided with a chic lounge bar. The result is Suzie's World. Beijing's glamour gang lounge around on traditional wooden beds piled high with silk cushions or settle themselves on giant couches and sip daiquiris. Suzie's is four floors and a

patio of opulent decor, friendly faces from around the globe, attentive table service and superb cocktails. The music is varied — house, chill-out, techno, pop and rock. It's like being at the house party of your dreams.

✉ **Chaoyang Amuse- ment Park (west gate, through Q Bar entrance)** ☎ 6593 7889 Ⓜ Dongsishitiao, then bus 115 ☾ 7pm-late

Bringing Down the Wall
If you're visiting Beijing in the summer, you could be in for the rave of your life. With 499 of your soon-to-be closest friends, party under the stars from dusk till dawn to tunes spun by the capital's top DJs, along with live music, art installations and film clips. The location? On top of the Great Wall of China. Despite sounding too fantastic to be true, the Henry Lee gang (of Neo Lounge, Vogue and Public Space) organise 24hr 'Illuminate the Great Wall' festivals each year. You may come away with a sprained ankle or two but you'll also experience the Great Wall in a whole new light. Check with listings magazines, Neo Lounge or 🖥 www.msgp.org for dates and details.

CINEMAS

Pirated DVDs and VCDs spill into Beijing so quickly that you can easily get your hands on films that have only had their US screen launch a day or two before. This does not do wonders for cinemas. To top it off, only a handful of Western films get the authorities' stamp of approval each year, making film-going for non-Chinese speakers somewhat dire. Nevertheless, if you're hungry for the big screen, the following cinemas are worth checking out.

Cherry Lane Theatre
(3, D13) Popular with expats, this theatre shows Chinese films with English subtitles every other Friday evening.
✉ **21st Century Theatre, 40 Liangmaqiao Lu**
☎ 6461 5318 🖳 www .cherrylanemovies.com.cn
🚌 402 💲 Y50

Goethe Institute Inter Nationes (3, D6)
Run, Lola, run to regular screenings of German movies with Chinese or English subtitles.
✉ **2 Xisanhuan Beilu**
☎ 6841 7891 ext 404
🚌 double-decker No 4

Lycee Francais de Pekin
(4, B15) If you like your films with a certain *je ne sais quoi*, this cinema-theque screens movies

from France.
✉ **13 Sanlitun Donsijie**
☎ 6532 3498
Ⓜ Dongzhimen

Sculpting In Time (3, B7)
Every Tuesday and Thursday, this place serves up classic films along with coffee and cakes.
✉ **7 Weigongcun Lu**
☎ 6894 6825
🚌 double-decker No 4
📅 Tues & Thurs evenings 💲 Y10

Star Expo Cinema (4, E9)
Most of the imported films that make it onto China's big screens pass through this cinema. It's a surprisingly little place but has big comfy chairs.
✉ **537 Dongsi Beidajie**
☎ 6527 4420
Ⓜ Dongdan, then bus 116

Sundong'an Cinema City
(4, G9) This cinema usually shows at least one Hollywood feature. If you're into Hong Kong flicks and can figure out the plot minus the subtitles, you've got a few of those to choose from as well.
✉ **5th fl, Dongan Shopping Centre, Wangfujing Dajie**
☎ 6528 1988
Ⓜ Wangfujing 💲 Y15

Universal Studios Experience (4, H11)
This is the place for big kids with kids. Cartoons and Western films are shown every Saturday and Sunday.
✉ **Henderson Centre, 18 Jianguomen Nei Dajie**
☎ 6518 3260 ext 207
Ⓜ Jianguomen ♿

Everybody is Kung Fu Fighting
For thousands of years, Chinese legends have told of women warriors. When kung fu hit the silver screen, these mythical female characters appeared with movie-star looks and lines. Ballet dancer Zhang Ziyi turned pirouettes into pounces and leapt from Beijing's stages to Hollywood's centre screen as the young, nasty girl in *Crouching Tiger, Hidden Dragon* and *Rush Hour 2*. She's fast, she's strong and she's China's newest *femme fatale*.

ROCK, JAZZ, BLUES & POP

Big Easy (3, E14)
The Big Easy has the feel of a Mississippi riverboat adrift in less than clean waters. With live jazz and blues, gumbo and blackened tuna steaks, it's a favourite with foreigners, despite drifting near sleazy shores.
✉ Chaoyang Amusement Park (south gate) ☎ 6508 6776 Ⓜ Dongsishitiao, then bus 115 🕙 5pm-2am

CD Café (4, C15)
This intimate, casual venue hosts Beijing's top bands. It leans heavily towards jazz but pop and rock make it on stage at least three nights a week. For popular bands, get here early. Call or check local listings magazines for details.
✉ C16 Dongsanhuan Beilu (south of Agricultural Centre)
☎ 6501 8877 ext 3032 Ⓜ Dongzhimen
🕙 8pm-2.30am
$ around Y30

Jam House (4, D14)
An old-timer on the Beijing bar scene, the Jam House stages regular rock and jazz. It's spacious and rarely gets claustrophobically crowded, and has one of the nicest rooftop terraces in town.
✉ Dongdaqiaoxie Jie (South Sanlitun Bar Street) ☎ 6506 3845 Ⓜ Dongsishitiao, then bus 113
🕙 7.30pm-2.30am

Nashville (4, D14)
Country and western style,

Going Solo
Chinese tend to go out en masse; the idea of going to the local bar alone (never mind one halfway around the world) is balked at by many locals. Unless you speak Chinese, finding yourself alone in a bar surrounded by crowds of people clinking *baijiu* can be a lonely experience. But it's not all so dire. Bars and clubs with a good mix of foreigners and locals have generally friendly, mingling crowds. Try the **World of Suzie Wong** (p85), **Poachers** (p83), **River Bar** (below), **La Rive Gauche** (p82) or the bars along the western shore of Qianhai Lake. **Frank's Place** (p83) and **Passby Bar** (p82) cater almost exclusively to foreigners and are good, nonpick-up places to meet people.

y'all can throw darts and have your choice of umpteen great beers on tap in this watering hole. It has boot-tappin' tunes on stage and a pop cover band performs now and again for good measure.
✉ Dongdaqiaoxie Jie (South Sanlitun Bar Street) ☎ 6502 4201 Ⓜ Dongsishitiao, then bus 113 🕙 6pm-2am

River Bar (4, D14)
This place has a rootsy, ethnic feel to it, with soft lighting, local art on the walls and low wooden tables and stools. A small stage hosts live folk rock from Wednesday to Saturday and impromptu jam sessions throughout the week.
✉ Dongdaqiaoxie Jie (South Sanlitun Bar Street) ☎ 6594 4714 Ⓜ Dongsishitiao, then bus 113 🕙 7pm-2am

Sergeant Pepper (3, E14)
With a pub-like interior and Beatle-mania dripping from the walls, this expat-befriended bar has live

Queuing at the River Bar

classic rock covered by a resident Filipino band.
✉ **Chaoyang Amusement Park (west gate)** ☎ 6500 8088 Ⓜ Dongsishitiao, then bus 115 ☽ 6pm-2am

Sound Stage (3, B8)
Simple, no frills and to the point, this venue offers live rock and metal bands. It has the best sound system in Beijing, as attested to by the students who regularly pack out the place.
✉ **A2 Huangtingzi Lu** ☎ 8204 8579 Ⓜ Jishuitan, then bus 902 ☽ 6.30pm-1.30am 💲 varies

Sweetness (3, D13)
Rock, pop and almost anything else you can think of finds its way onto the stage here. Enjoy it with some micro-brewed beer.
✉ **19 Liangmaqiao Lu** ☎ 8456 2899 🚌 402 ☽ 11am-late 💲 varies

THEATRE

Going to the theatre can set you back the price of a bowl of noodles or nearly as much as your hotel room. Prices vary dramatically, depending on who takes the stage. Always call in advance to check.

Capital Theatre (4, E9)
Contemporary Chinese productions can be seen here six days a week. Call for a schedule.
✉ **22 Wangfujing Dajie** ☎ 6524 9847 Ⓜ Wangfujing ☽ Tues-Sun 7pm

Central Academy of Drama Theatre (4, C8)
The academy's students regularly perform here. This is where Gong Li and Zhang Ziyi, big names on the big screen, learned their art.
✉ **39 Dongnianhua Hutong** ☎ 6401 3959 Ⓜ Andingmen, then bus 108

Central Experimental Drama Theatre (4, C7)
Regular avant-garde theatre for culture vultures.

✉ **A45 Mao'er Hutong** ☎ 6403 1099

Chang'an Grand Theatre (4, H11) While opera tends to get centre stage here, the theatre occasionally puts on classical Chinese plays.
✉ **7 Jianguomen Nei Dajie** ☎ 6510 1309 Ⓜ Jianguomen

People's Art Theatre (4, E9) Find out who's walking the floorboards of Beijing's thespian scene by taking in one of the People's regular performances.
✉ **22 Wangfujing Dajie** ☎ 6525 0123 Ⓜ Wangfujing

Play Bar (4, J3)
If you've got a real zeal for theatre, head to this tavern devoted to Beijing's contemporary drama.
✉ **81 Xuanwumen Xidajie** ☎ 6607 9184 Ⓜ Xuanwumen ☽ noon-1am

The Capital Theatre by night

Actors in costume – looks serious but it's all good fun

CLASSICAL MUSIC

21st Century Theatre
(3, D13) The violin, cello and flute get centre stage here with top symphony orchestras.
✉ 40 Liangmaqiao Lu
☎ 6366 4805 🚌 402
☾ usually 7.30pm
💲 Y50-800

Beijing Concert Hall
(4, H4) This elaborate concert hall has nightly performances of classical Chinese music as well as international repertoires.
✉ 1 Beixinhua Jie
☎ 6605 5812
Ⓜ Xidan ☾ usually 7.30pm 💲 Y50-500

Forbidden City Concert Hall (4, G6)
Set in Zhongshan Park,

this concert hall showcases classical and traditional Chinese music nightly.
✉ **Zhongshan Park**
☎ 6559 8294
Ⓜ Tiananmen Xi
☾ usually 7.30pm
💲 Y50-500

National Library Concert Hall (3, E6)
New interpretations of classical Chinese tunes as well as classical pieces from around the world are performed here.
✉ 33 Zhongguancun Nandajie ☎ 6848 5462
Ⓜ Xizhimen
☾ usually 7.30pm
💲 Y10-300

Poly Plaza International Theatre (4, C12)
You can find a wide range

of classical music performances here, from Chinese folk to the China Philharmonic Orchestra.
✉ **Poly Plaza, 14 Dongzhimen Nandajie**
☎ 6500 1188 ext 5127
Ⓜ Dongsishitiao
☾ usually 7.30pm
💲 Y80-480

Sanwei Bookstore & Teahouse (4, H3)
After browsing through the small bookshop, head upstairs to the teahouse for live traditional Chinese music every Saturday night.
✉ 60 Fuxingmen Nei Dajie ☎ 6601 3204
Ⓜ Xidan ☾ 8pm
💲 Y30

ACROBATICS & KUNG FU

Chaoyang Theatre
(4, E15) Visiting acrobatic troupes fill the stage with plate-spinning and hoop-jumping.
✉ **36 Dongsanhuan Beilu** ☎ 6507 2421 Ⓜ Chaoyangmen, then bus 101 ⌚ 7.30pm ⓢ Y80 ♿

Dongyue Temple (4, E13)
In the back courtyard of Dongyue Temple, enjoy tea, snacks and acrobatics under the early morning sky. It supposedly takes place year-round, but you'd best call before you set your alarm (especially in winter).
✉ **Chaoyangmen Wai Dajie** ☎ 6553 2184 Ⓜ Chaoyangmen ⌚ 8am ⓢ Y60

Heaven & Earth Theatre
(4, C12) Young performers from the China Acrobatic Circus mesmerise the crowd with joint-popping, mind-bending routines. This is a favourite with tour groups so book ahead. You can also visit the circus school to see the performers training (☎ 6502 3984).
✉ **10 Dongzhimen Nandajie** ☎ 6416 9893 Ⓜ Dongsishitiao ⌚ 7.15pm ⓢ Y120 (no credit cards accepted) ♿

Liyuan Theatre (3, H9)
Over the centuries, the monks of Songshan Mountain Temple have developed 'Shaoling Kung Fu' to protect their sacred

grounds. The performance here demonstrates these ancient moves to a lunch-munching crowd.
✉ **Jianguo Hotel Qianmen, 175 Yong'an Lu** ☎ 8315 7297, 6301 6688 ext 8822 Ⓜ Hepingmen, then any bus south ⌚ 12.30pm; box office 9am-8pm ⓢ Y80 (incl lunch)

Wansheng Theatre
(6, C1) The Beijing Acrobatics Troupe is considered to give the best acrobatic performance in Beijing. Catch it nightly.
✉ **Beiwei Lu** ☎ 6303 7449 Ⓜ Qianmen ⌚ 7.15pm ⓢ Y100-150 ♿

OPERA

Chang'an Grand Theatre
(4, H11) Come here for an authentic Chinese opera experience. Members of the audience chatter knowledgably and slurp tea loudly while the stage is filled with giant operatic presences.
✉ **7 Jianguomen Nei Dajie** ☎ 6510 1309 Ⓜ Jianguomen ⌚ 7.15pm ⓢ Y20-120

Huguang Guild Hall
(3, H9) Elaborately decorated with balconies surrounding the canopied stage, this theatre hosts nightly Beijing opera performances. It's also the site where the Kuomintang was established in 1912.

✉ **3 Hufangqiao Lu** ☎ 6351 8284 Ⓜ Hepingmen ⌚ 7.15pm ⓢ Y60-180

Lao She Teahouse (4, K6)
The performances here are a combination of opera, crosstalk and acrobatics.
✉ **3rd fl, 3 Qianmen Xidajie** ☎ 6303 6380 Ⓜ Qianmen ⌚ 7.30pm, occasional shows 3pm ⓢ Y60-130

Liyuan Theatre (3, H9)
Traditional operas are staged each night in this far from traditional setting.
✉ **Jianguo Hotel Qianmen, 175 Yong'an Lu** ☎ 8315 7297,

6301 6688 ext 8822 Ⓜ Hepingmen, then any bus south ⌚ 7.30pm; box office 9am-8pm ⓢ Y30-150

Prince Gong's Residence
(4, C5) The gorgeous Grand Opera House in the west of this residency dates back to the Qing dynasty and is a fantastic place to appreciate traditional Beijing opera. It's a good idea to reserve.
✉ **14 Liuyin Jie** ☎ 6618 6628 Ⓜ Gulou Dajie, then taxi southwest ⌚ Jul-Oct 7.30pm, Nov-June call for schedule ⓢ Y60 (incl tea & snacks)

Colourful Characters

Unable to follow those piercing voices? Still trying to figure out who's who? Don't despair; there is a clue to help you distinguish the naughty characters from the nice on the Beijing opera stage. Just check out the colour of the performers' make-up. The one in black is the honest, good guy while the character wearing white is crafty and cunning. Red make-up signifies loyalty and honour, blue means courage and adventure, and yellow is used for the clever and gentle character. And the colourful character slurping tea and cracking sunflower seeds? She's just a member of the audience.

KEREN SU / CHINA SPAN

Zhengyi Ci Theatre
(4, K5) Originally a temple, China's oldest wooden theatre is ornately decorated and a superb place to experience Beijing opera. The theatre was bought privately, restored and revived in 1995 and has been going strong ever since.
✉ 220 Qianmen Xiheyan Jie ☎ 8315 3150 M Hepingmen
🕒 7.30pm $ Y80-280

GAY & LESBIAN BEIJING

In 2001 the Chinese Psychiatric Association finally declassified homosexuality as a mental disorder. Nevertheless, authorities continue to take a dim view of homosexuality, considering it a 'Western problem'. As a gay foreigner in China you are a potential target for discrimination. While very unlikely, it is not beyond the authorities to send you packing if you display overt homosexual behaviour in public. Beijing does have a growing gay scene to which the authorities generally turn a blind eye and, although it's still largely underground, clubs are beginning to advertise gay and lesbian nights. You can check 🖥 www.utopia-asia.com/tipschin.htm for tips on where to go.

Half & Half (4, C14)
Small but popular, this unassuming gay bar is patronised by a devoted group of regulars.
✉ 15 Sanlitun Lu
☎ 6416 6919
M Dongsishitiao, then bus 113 🕒 7pm-2am

JJ (4, B3)
While it's largely straight, this club does draw a gay crowd. On weekends it packs in dancers for its glitter-pop remixes.
✉ 74-76 Xinjiekou Beidajie ☎ 6618 9305 M Jishuitan 🕒 8pm-4am $ Y20-50

On Off Bar (4, C13)
Low lighting, comfy lounge seating and jazzy ambient music make this a nice, intimate place for a drink. It's frequented by gay crowds and on Thursday night the dance party is exclusively for lesbians.
✉ 5 Xingfuyicun Lu
☎ 6415 8083
M Dongzhimen 🕒 10am-2am $ varies

Orange (4, C13)
This trendy, atmospheric dance club hosts regular lesbian and gay parties (usually on Saturday). DJs play R&B, hip-hop, dance and chill-out.
✉ 2-10 Xingfu Yicun (alley across from Workers' Stadium, north entrance) ☎ 6415 7413 M Dongsishitiao, then any bus east 🕒 9pm-3am $ free-Y20

SPECTATOR SPORTS

With the exception of football, ask a Beijinger where you can see some sports and you'll be given a perplexed shrug of the shoulder. A sports-bar waiter will simply point at the TV. At the moment, spectator sports are absent on the Beijing scene but it can only be assumed that, as the 2008 Olympics approach, this will all change. Keep your eyes on the **National Olympic Sports Centre** (1 Anding Lu; 3, B10).

Football

The Chinese wowed themselves by making it into the FIFA World Cup and Beijingers have gone football crazy, packing out the stadiums. National games are played at the Workers' Stadium on Sunday and Wednesday (Gongren Tiyuchang Beilu; 4, D13; ☎ 6502 5757). You can buy tickets (Y100) at the north entrance a couple of days before each match or from hawkers around the stadium on game night.

T'ai Chi

Technically t'ai chi is not a spectator sport, but it is the thing that gets Beijingers up and out in the morning with a string of interested tourists behind them. The ancient art form is about energy flow and, while it looks like practitioners are going about it in slow motion, it is also a form of self-defence. Judging from the folks you see bending and stretching, it will also keep you limber well into your nineties. Good places to see t'ai chi early in the morning are Jingshan Park (p32), Taoranting Park (p39) and Temple of Heaven Park (p14).

Olympic Mania

It won't be long before you see signs of it everywhere. Beijing has been granted the Olympics for 2008 and the city is ignited with excitement. Posters are up, banners are hung, athletic teams are priming themselves and the day of the official 'You Won' announcement has become an annual celebration. A giant new complex is in the works and creativity is seeping through to the government, evident through unlikely proposals such as hosting the volleyball competition in Tiananmen Square (!!). The mood is elated, and Beijing's Olympic machine is in full swing, busy designing the logo, pumping out T-shirts, landscaping new parks and giving the city the biggest spring-clean it's ever seen.

Sleeping

Hotels are almost as common as chopsticks in Beijing. However, as a foreigner, many of these – particularly mid-range and budget options – are off-limits to you. The licence that hotels must hold in order to accommodate foreigners is most often granted to chains and top-end places. That said, there are a growing number of excellent options for every wallet size.

Never assume the hotel's listed rates are its actual prices. Many hotels often slash these by 40% to 50% in all but the busiest times of the year. The peak season for Chinese tourists is July and August, when mid-range and budget hotels are very busy. The high season for foreign travellers is September and October, when top-end hotels tend to fill up and charge closer to their posted rates. In the dead of winter you can often bargain fantastic deals in all hotels. If you're going to be in Beijing over Chinese New Year, book ahead, as many hotels close down.

> ### Room Rates
> These categories indicate the cost per night of a standard double room.
>
> | | |
> |---|---|
> | Deluxe | Y1650 and over |
> | Top End | Y1000-1649 |
> | Mid-Range | Y500-999 |
> | Budget | Y499 and under |
>
> Deluxe and top-end hotels add a 15% service charge to quoted rates.

Beijing's deluxe hotels provide the full services and amenities you would expect in the West for a fraction of the price. They offer airport shuttles, tours, business services, Internet access, pools, gyms, bars and restaurants. They're so like Western hotels you'd never guess you'd left home. This can be a plus for those looking for familiarity but a bit of a disappointment for those looking for something with a flavour of China. Top-end hotels often have far more Chinese character.

Mid-range and budget hotels offer fewer amenities and are often somewhat frayed around the edges. However, a number of the city's atmospheric courtyard hotels fall within this price range. With excellent service and steeped in history, these are the most unique accommodation options. For travellers on a shoestring, there aren't scores of options, but what's available is clean and comfortable. Dorm-room accommodation will set you back Y60-100.

The grand entrance to the deluxe Grand Hyatt Beijing

DELUXE

Ascott (3, G13)

This very chic hotel offers terrific, discrete service; an excellent business centre with secretarial, limousine and courier services; and a fully equipped gym. There is also a children's playground, a doctor on call and babysitting services for those travelling with a brood. Well located opposite the China World Trade Centre, it has a sophisticated air about it without being flashy.

✉ 2 Donghuan Nanlu ☎ 6567 8100; fax 6567 8122 ⌨ www.the -ascott.com Ⓜ Guo Mao ✗ Taj Pavilion (p74), Henry J Bean's (p73) ♿

China World Hotel

(4, H15) Luxury without stuffiness, this newly renovated Shangri-la giant offers bright and comfy standard rooms, an array of suites and all the amenities you can think of. It also has lots of well-equipped function rooms.

✉ 1 Jianguomen Wai Dajie ☎ 6505 2266; fax 6505 0828 ⌨ cwh@ shangri-la.com Ⓜ Guo

Mao ✗ Taj Pavilion (p74), Henry J Bean's (p73)

Grand Hyatt Beijing

(4, H9) This hotel is so gorgeous you may have a hard time tearing yourself away from your room. Thankfully, many of the city's major sights are only a few minutes from the door. There's an indoor pool with a virtual sky, a kiddie's pool and play area, and an attached shopping centre. Every room has floor-to-ceiling windows and marble bathrooms and you can enjoy evening cocktails before being whisked to the airport by limo.

✉ Oriental Plaza, 1 Dongchang'an Jie ☎ 8518 1234; fax 8518 0000 ⌨ www.hyatt.com Ⓜ Wangfujing ✗ Scholtzsky's Deli (p72), The Courtyard (p70) ♿

Kerry Centre Hotel

(4, G15) With stylish decor and good business services, this Shangri-la hotel is justifiably popular with business travellers. There are a number of smart

Lobby of the Palace Hotel

dining options within the hotel and the Kerry Centre shopping mall is adjacent.

✉ 1 Guanghua Lu ☎ 6561 8833; fax 6561 2626 ⌨ www.shangri -la.com Ⓜ Guo Mao ♿

Palace Hotel (4, G9)

In the opulent Art Deco lobby, classy music floats between Tiffany's and Christian Dior. Upstairs, the standard rooms are a bit cramped and not quite as ultra-luxurious as you might expect, however, the service is stellar and the location and amenities are tops.

✉ 8 Jinyu Hutong ☎ 6559 2888; fax 6512 9050 ⌨ www.peninsula .com Ⓜ Dongdan ✗ The Courtyard (p70)

St Regis (4, H12)

Elegance and professionalism make this one of Beijing's top hotels. Rooms are exactly what you expect of a deluxe hotel – graceful and luxurious – and the staff are friendly and helpful. Offerings include a putting range and aromatherapy facials.

✉ 21 Jianguomen Wai Dajie ☎ 6460 6688; fax 6460 3299 ⌨ www .stregis.com/beijing Ⓜ Jianguomen ✗ Danieli's (p73)

Room Hunting

If you arrive in town with nowhere to stay, staff at the information booth at the airport can help you out. They can get you bargains at many well-known hotels as well as rooms in budget to mid-range hotels that can't normally accept foreigners. They'll even get you on the right bus into town. If you'd rather book before you arrive, check out ⌨ www.sinohotel.com, where it's a breeze to book rooms and airport-to-hotel transfers.

TOP END

Asia Hotel (4, C12)
Despite the rather dull exterior, you can't do better than this. The service is flawless and the rooms are plush and impeccably decorated, with a Chinese touch. Inside are some of Beijing's top restaurants and it's well located near the nightlife and the subway.
✉ 8 Xinzhong Xijie, off Gongren Tiyuchang Beilu ☎ 6500 7788; fax 6500 8001 🖳 sales@bj-asia hotel.com.cn Ⓜ Dong-sishitiao 🍴 Old Dock (p67), Cherry Tree Café (p66) 🛂

Beijing Hotel (4, H8)
Dating back to 1900, Beijing's oldest hotel has been refurbished and once again boasts some of the city's most fabulous rooms. The deluxe rooms have views across Tiananmen Square and the Forbidden City. There are countless restaurants within the hotel and it's steps away from the Wangfujing shopping district.
✉ 33 Dongchang'an Jie

☎ 6513 7766 ext 777; fax 6523 2395 🖳 business@china beijinghotel.com.cn Ⓜ Wangfujing 🍴 Gonin Byakusho (p70), Wangfujing Snack Street (p72)

Grand Hotel (4, H8)
With the city's best views over the golden rooftops of the Forbidden City, the spacious rooms here are decorated with traditional, wooden Chinese furniture. The 1st-floor lounge has a 1930s feel about it.
✉ 35 Dongchang'an Jie ☎ 6513 0057; fax 6513 0050 🖳 www.grand hotelbeijing.com Ⓜ Tiananmen Dong 🍴 The Courtyard (p70)

Jinglun (4, H14)
While not likely your first choice, this hotel is well located and, as it's extremely popular with Chinese tourists, it may be quieter in autumn than some of its competitors. Rooms are nice but nothing special and the lobby is a hive of activity.
✉ 3 Jianguomen Wai Dajie ☎ 6500 2266; fax 6500 2022 🖳 www .jinglunhotel.com Ⓜ Yong An Li 🍴 Justine's (p73)

Kempinski Hotel (3, D13)
Rated as one of the city's top hotels, its spacious, swish rooms have street or river views. Service is excellent and, attached to the Youyi Lufthansa Centre,

the amenities are endless. You can get some great deals here.
✉ 50 Liangmaqiao Lu ☎ 6465 3388; fax 6465 3366 Ⓜ Guo Mao, then bus 207 🍴 Red Basil (p77), Trattoria La Gondola (p78)

Movenpick (1, C3)
If you're only on a brief stopover in Beijing and have an early departure, this four-star hotel has excellent amenities, including tennis courts and a huge outdoor pool, and is neighbours with the airport.
✉ Capital International Airport ☎ 6456 5588; fax 6456 5678 🍴 hotel shuttles into town

Poly Plaza Hotel (4, C12)
The rooms here are comfortable although not at all distinct. Staff are friendly and very helpful and the location is great.
✉ 14 Dongzhimen Nandajie ☎ 6500 1188; fax 6501 0268 🖳 salespolyplaza@ 163.net Ⓜ Dong-sishitiao 🍴 Sunset Terrace (p68)

Presidential Plaza (3, F8)
This hotel caters to business travellers, with excellent business services, and has lovely, home-away-from-home rooms. Service is flawless.
✉ 9 Fuchengmen Wai Lu ☎ 6800 5588; fax 6800 5888 🖳 www .stateguesthotel.com Ⓜ Fuchengmen

Red Capital Residence
(4, D10) By far Beijing's most atmospheric hotel, this place oozes with retro-kitsch communist decor. Stay in the chairman's suite, a concubine's boudoir or an author's study. The Bomb Shelter Bar, accessed through a rockery in the courtyard, plays Long March propaganda films and serves cigars and port. It all cleverly teeters on the burlesque and is so worth a visit.

✉ 9 Dongsi Liutiao ☎ 6402 7150, 8403 5308; fax 8403 5303 💻 www.redcapital club.com.cn Ⓜ Dong-sishitiao, then bus 115 or 118 ✗ Red Capital Club (p72)

Swissotel (4, C12)
This five-star hotel has top business services and a good location, but the rooms are nothing special and the service is snobbish.

Nevertheless, it continues to draw crowds from far and wide.

✉ 2 Chaoyangmen Beidajie ☎ 6501 2288; fax 6501 2501 💻 www .swissotel.com Ⓜ Dong-sishitiao ✗ Sunset Terrace (p68)

Wangfujing Grand (4, E8)
This place is fabulously located between the Wangfujing shopping district and the Forbidden City. The service is very friendly but the rooms are beginning to feel just that tiny bit worn.

✉ 57 Wangfujing Dajie ☎ 6522 1188; fax 6522 3749 💻 www.wang fujinghotel.com Ⓜ Wangfujing ✗ The Courtyard (p70)

Atmosphere abounds at Red Capital Residence

MID-RANGE

Comfort Inn (4, C15)
This well-located, new hotel has clean and comfortable, though fairly nondescript, rooms. Bonuses include discounts for kids and seniors with reservations, rooms designed for disabled guests and a top-floor pool.
✉ 4 Gongren Tiyuchang Beilu ☎ 8523 5522; fax 8523 5577 💻 www .choicehotels.com Ⓜ Dongsishitiao, then bus 113 ✗ Serve the People (p76), Mediterraneo (p76) ♿

Friendship Guesthouse
(4, C8) Built in 1875, this large courtyard hotel was home to Chiang Kai-shek in

the 1940s. At the time of writing it was being refurbished and has comfortable rooms encircling small gardens and pavilions.
✉ 7 Houyuan Hutong ☎ 6403 1114; fax 6401 4603 Ⓜ Andingmen

Friendship Hotel (3, D6)
Built in the 1950s to house 'foreign experts', this sprawling garden-style hotel retains its old-world charm and has lovely rooms and a fantastic outdoor pool. It's a bit of a trek from downtown but its

Old-world charm of the Friendship Hotel

popularity persists with both foreigners and Chinese tourists.

✉ 1 Zhongguancun Nandajie ☎ 6849 8080; fax 6849 8866 🖳 www .cbw.com/hotel/friendship 🚌 double-decker No 4 🍴 Away (p78), Jiuhuashan Roast Duck Restaurant (p78)

Holiday Inn Lido (3, C14) Beijing's most kid-friendly hotel has bowling, Baskin-Robbins ice cream, a pool, babysitting, and packed lunches from the deli. It's far from downtown but has regular shuttles and tours. The rooms are clean, comfortable and very much like Holiday Inns around the globe. There's no hushed glamour to this place but it's relaxed and full of conveniences.

✉ Jichang Lu ☎ 6437 6688; fax 6437 6237 🖳 www.lidoplace.com 🚌 shuttle to & from downtown & the airport 🚶

Jianguo Hotel Beijing (4, H14) This relaxed hotel is only a few storeys high and, with a stream running through its minicourtyard garden, it's a cosy escape from the hectic road outside. Its rooms are a little yesteryear but it's extremely popular; don't bother with the deluxe suites as they're not worth the asking price. Book ahead as this place is often full.

✉ 5 Jianguomen Wai Dajie ☎ 6500 2233; fax 6500 2871 🖳 www .hoteljianguo.com

The relaxing indoor garden at Jianguo Hotel Beijing

Ⓜ Yong An Li 🍴 Justine's (p73)

Jianguo Hotel Qianmen (3, H9) The rooms here look as though they've recently been refurbished and are much more bright and pleasant than the slightly garish lobby. The staff are helpful although often busy with tour groups. This is a good mid-range option.

✉ 175 Yong'an Lu ☎ 6301 6688; fax 6301 3883 Ⓜ Hepingmen, then any bus south

Jianguo Inn (4, A15) This inn has the feel of an American motel. Rooms are clean, bright, basic and excellent value.

✉ 8 Xinyuan Nanlu ☎ 6597 1866 Ⓜ Dongzhimen

🍴 Belle Vue (p77), Red Basil (p77)

Lusonguan Binguan (4, C8) This hotel has beautiful, traditionally decorated rooms opening onto private terraces and gardens. Down a small *hutong*, it's a peaceful escape.

✉ 22 Banchang Hutong ☎ 6404 0436; fax 6403 0418 🖳 lsyhotel@263 .net Ⓜ Andingmen

Novotel Xinqiao Hotel (4, J9) The lobby can get boisterous but the rooms in this hotel are bright and comfortable. It's popular with Chinese tourists and fills up fast, so book ahead.

✉ Chongwenmen Xidajie ☎ 6513 3366; fax 6512 5126 🖳 gmanag er@novotelxinqiaobj.com Ⓜ Chongwenmen

Staying Awhile?
If you're looking for a serviced apartment, there are a number of good options in town. **Ascott** (p94) has two-, three- and four-bedroom deluxe flats, where you will be genuinely pampered (Y2320-6630/day). Spacious two- and three-bedroom flats at the **Asia Hotel** (p95) have kitchen facilities (Y3315/8300 day/week) and the giant suites at the **Red House Hotel** (p98) include kitchenettes and laundry facilities (Y300/day). Rates for serviced apartments are reduced if you book for a full month.

BUDGET

Bamboo Garden Hotel (Zhuyuang Binguan)

(4, A6) This tranquil courtyard hotel dates back to the Qing dynasty. The gardens belonged to a eunuch in Empress Cixi's entourage. Rooms are traditionally decorated and each has a balcony over the green and somewhat unkempt grounds. Rates are at the top end of the budget range.

✉ 24 Xiaoshiqiao Hutong ☎ 6403 2229; fax 6401 2633 ▯ www.bbgh.com.cn Ⓜ Gulou Dajie

Beijing International Hostel (Guoji Qingnian Lushe) (4, H11)

Clean, bright and quiet and in an excellent, central location, this hostel has aircon, 24hr hot water, bike rental and Internet access. It's definitely a young backpackers' hangout, with the feel of a college dorm, and offers bunks in eight-person rooms or doubles. Washrooms are communal.

✉ 9 Jianguomen Nei Dajie ☎ 6512 6688 ext 6145; fax 6522 9494 ▯ BIH-YH@sohu.com Ⓜ Jianguomen

Far East International Youth Hostel (Yuandong Guoji Qingnian Lushe) (3, H9)

Beijing's best dorm accommodation is in this courtyard hostel. Down deep in the *hutongs*, it's full of character, has clean rooms and kitchen facilities. Guests can relax and swap travelling stories in the quiet courtyard.

✉ 90 Tieshu Xiejie ☎ 6301 8811 ext 3118; fax 6301 8233 Ⓜ Hepingmen

Haoyuan Binguan (4, F10)

Along a quiet *hutong* and guarded by two stone lions, this courtyard hotel was once the residence of a eunuch. The standard rooms are lovely, with traditional decor, and the deluxe rooms are sumptuous. Rates are remarkable – this is definitely a mid- to top-end hotel. Try to get a room in the peaceful back courtyard.

✉ 53 Shijia Hutong ☎ 6512 5557; fax 6535 3179 Ⓜ Dongdan ✖ Green Tianshi Vegetarian Restaurant (p71)

Lusonguan Binguan

(4, C8) This peaceful hotel (see p97) also has excellent dorm accommodation.

✉ 22 Banchang Hutong ☎ 6404 0436; fax 6403 0418 ▯ lsyhotel@263 .net Ⓜ Andingmen

Poacher's Inn Youth Hostel (4, C14)

You like the nightlife? You like to party? This dorm accommodation lacks character but it's right in the heart of Sanlitun and attached to one of the most popular pubs in town. The eight-bed rooms are clean, but don't expect quiet.

✉ 43 Beisanlitun Lu, off Sanlitun Lu ☎ 6417 2632, 6417 2597; fax 6415 6866 ▯ www

Haoyuan Binguan

.poachers.com.cn Ⓜ Dongsishitiao, then bus 113 ✖ Golden Elephant (p75)

Qiaoyuan Fandian (3, J9)

It's lost in the southern suburbs but this dorm-style hotel is exceptionally popular with our backpacking readers. There's bike rental, laundry facilities, Internet access and a tourist information office.

✉ 135 You'anmen Dongbinhe Lu ☎ 6301 2244; fax 6303 0119 Ⓜ Qianmen, then bus 106

Red House Hotel (Ruixiu Binguan) (4, B13)

A great location and fairly quiet, this hotel doesn't have much atmosphere but the vast, air-conditioned suites are a bargain. Dorms are clean, Internet access is available and the staff are friendly and helpful.

✉ 10 Chunxiu Lu ☎ 6416 7810, 6416 7500; fax 6416 7600 ▯ www.redhouse.com.cn Ⓜ Dongzhimen ✖ Lemongrass (p66)

About Beijing

HISTORY
Long, Long Ago

Peking Man, believed to be one of the first people to call earth home, dwelled in the neighbourhood of Beijing some 500,000 years ago. The earliest recorded settlement in this area dates from about 1000BC, after which Beijing quickly developed as a frontier trading town for Mongols, Koreans and tribes of people now known as China's ethnic minorities. Positioned on the edge of the North China Plain, the city became a strategic pawn during the Warring States period (475-221BC) and conquerors began to quarrel over it. In AD1215 Genghis Khan, the great Mongol warrior, descended on the city; his grandson Kublai eventually became ruler of the largest empire the world's ever known, with Beijing (then known as Dadu) as its capital. This was China's Yuan dynasty (1279-1368), brought to an end by the world's first case of paper-currency inflation, topped with a few natural disasters.

Imperial Heyday

The Ming dynasty (1368-1644) saw the city and its walls refurbished and the Forbidden City and Temple of Heaven erected. The basic grid of present-day Beijing was born. The Mings also overhauled the Great Wall in an attempt to keep out the Manchus, who waltzed into town anyway, overthrew the Mings and established the Qing dynasty (1644-1911). The Qings further renovated the city and added summer palaces, pagodas and temples. During the final years of Qing rule, invaders and rebels launched repeated strikes against Beijing. The Second Opium War (1856-60), the Taiping Rebellion (1851-64) and the Boxer Rebellion (1900; see boxed text above) all took their toll on the capital, as did the Qing's last true leader, Empress Dowager Cixi (see the boxed text p13).

> **Boxed Up**
> Culled from secret societies, the Boxers were a xenophobic group who erupted in rebellion at the end of the 19th century with violent attacks on missionaries and their families. Tired of the foreigners themselves, the Qing Court decided to support the Boxers. Armed with this backing and with charms and martial-arts techniques that they believed made them impervious to Western bullets, the Boxers began massacring foreigners at random and the famous 50-day siege of Beijing's Foreign Legations began. It wasn't long before Western allies landed, handed the Qing Court a crippling foreign debt and knocked the Boxers down for the count.

Revolt!

When Cixi died, she bequeathed power to two-year-old Puyi, China's last emperor. The Qing dynasty, brutal and incompetent at the best of times, was now rudderless and it quickly collapsed. The revolution of 1911 paved the way for the Kuomintang to take power and the Republic of China was declared, with Sun Yatsen as president. Warlords continued to carve and rule the north of the country and foreigners controlled important economic zones in major ports like Shanghai and Tianjin.

Crippling poverty and splintered rule was a recipe for further rebellion. Beijing University bubbled with dissent and it was here that Karl Marx's *The Communist Manifesto* found its way into the hands of a library assistant named Mao Zedong (1893-1976). The Communists soon emerged and pensively joined with the Kuomintang to wrestle power from the northern warlords. The Kuomintang turned on the Communists a year later (1927) and slaughtered them en masse. Communist survivors fled to the countryside and launched a civil war.

The Japanese invaded Beijing in 1937 and overran the east of China for the duration of WWII, causing the Kuomintang to flee west. After Japan's defeat by Allied forces in 1945, the Kuomintang returned to Beijing but its days were numbered; by this time the Chinese Civil War was in full swing and the Communists, under the leadership of Mao, cheered victory in 1949. As the Kuomintang fled to Taiwan, the People's Liberation Army (PLA) marched into Beijing, where Mao proclaimed the People's Republic of China.

Aftermath

After 1949 came a period of catastrophic historical destruction in Beijing. The huge city walls were pulled down, hundreds of temples and monuments were destroyed and buildings were flattened. In 1966 Mao launched the Cultural Revolution and China was to

On guard at Tiananmen

remain in the grip of chaos for a decade. Anything considered antiproletarian was destroyed – from temples to the education system to countless people. Everyone became suspect of harbouring 'capitalist-roadster' thoughts, neighbours turned on one another and Mao's youth army, the Red Guard, terrorised the nation.

In 1979 the pragmatic Deng Xiaoping, a former protégé of Mao, launched a modernisation drive. The country opened up and Westerners were given the chance to see what the Communists had been up to for the past 30 years. The 1980s and 90s saw the restoration of temples, monuments and schools. Glittering towers and high-rises erupted. China decided to embrace modernity without altering politically. In 1989 pro-democracy student demonstrations took place in Tiananmen Square; the government's brutal retaliation sent shivers through the world. Today, there's a conspicuous absence of protest in Beijing. Political dissent exists, but unrelenting government coercion has consigned it to a deeply subterranean level. Somehow, Beijing is riding two very different currents – communism and capitalism – into this new century.

ORIENTATION

Mountainous along the north and west, and flat in the southeast, Beijing municipality stretches 16,800 sq km, with the city limits extending some 80km. The capital was originally built along a north–south axis, with temples and buildings organised symmetrically. The Temple of Heaven is at the southern end of the axis, Ditan Park is in the north and between them lay many of the city's main attractions.

Map Terms		
road	lu	路
street	jie	街
avenue	dajie	大街
boulevard	dadao	大道
alley	hutong	胡同
lane	xiang	巷
inner	nei	内
outer	wai	外
north	bei	北
south	nan	南
east	dong	东
west	xi	西
village	li	里
gate	men	门
bridge	qiao	桥

Beijing is divided into 10 districts: in the south, Chongwen and Xuanwu are largely residential; in the centre, Dongcheng and Xicheng are where much of old Beijing and its *hutongs* can be found; to the east, Chaoyang District encompasses the expat neighbourhoods of Sanlitun and Jianguomen; and to the far northwest, Haidian is home to the zoo, universities and summer palaces. Ringed by four major roads and crisscrossed by wide boulevards, navigating downtown is relatively simple – until you enter the maze of *hutongs* between the thoroughfares.

Many of Beijing's buildings are unnumbered and use addresses such as 'next to 114' or 'across from City Hotel'. Street names change at each major intersection, adding a direction or point of reference; when you're hunting down a Beijing location, a little Chinese terminology can take you a long way (see the boxed text above).

ENVIRONMENT

With one of the world's largest populations and a rapidly expanding economy, Beijing's environment feels the strain. While some days the smog can clog your lungs and wafts from drains can nearly asphyxiate you, Beijing is making an effort to clean up its act. Recycling bins dot Tiananmen Square, officials

The Green Wall of China

If you visit Beijing in spring and experience the sand storms that send residents rushing around with plastic bags over their heads, you may not be so surprised to hear that the city may one day be swallowed up by the Gobi Desert. Only 18km away, the winds are blowing the sands towards the capital at a rate of 2km a year, with 30m dunes closing in. Experts blame overgrazing and deforestation; every month 200 sq km of arable land in China becomes desert. China's government has pledged US$6.8 billion to build a green wall between Beijing and the sands; at 5700km long, it will be longer than the Great Wall of China.

Enjoying the greenery of a Beijing park

trumpet a target of 90% of buses and 70% of taxis to be running on natural gas by 2007, and industries prone to pollution are being relocated out into the suburbs. China's entry into the World Trade Organization (WTO) and an Olympic mandate to purify the air before 2008 are largely responsible for Beijing's sudden green campaign. Beijing also boasts an increasing number of lush green spaces; however, with water resources stretched to their limits and drought taking over much of the country, residents (and visitors) are urged to conserve every last drop.

GOVERNMENT & POLITICS

Communist by name if not entirely by nature, China's central government has its quarters in Beijing, although precious little is known about its inner workings. Political competition is not tolerated in China and political debate in public has long been a dangerous and therefore infrequent activity. Beijing is an independent municipality within Hubei province, with its own mayor, however, like many national capitals, the municipality is directly under the control of the central government.

ECONOMY

After two decades of intense development, China's current annual economic growth of 7% to 8% is considered relatively slow. While the number of shops and shoppers in Beijing make the economic picture look shiny and bright, unemployment is on the rise and you will encounter the urban poor as well as the rural poor who have taken to the city in an attempt to find work.

Increasingly, state-owned enterprises are being bought out or shut down; many of the laid-off workers feel the government has abandoned them to the market economy, and social unrest is beginning to rumble. In an attempt to stimulate the economy, the government is pouring money into public-works projects and welcoming foreign investment with open arms. While some predict that the Chinese economy will be the world's largest by 2020, it's difficult to know what the true picture really is: mass corruption leads to catastrophically inaccurate statistics and also sends around 13% to 17% of China's GDP into unlawful ends.

Did You Know?

- Beijing's population is 13.075 million
- The population density in Beijing is 659 per sq km
- There are 84,000 tourist hotel rooms and 5000 tourist guides
- There is 9.7 sq m of public green space for each resident
- 8564 theatrical and art performances take place each year
- 2.66 million Beijingers are mobile-phone subscribers

SOCIETY & CULTURE

Over 95% of Beijingers are Han Chinese, with only a scattering of representatives from China's 56 official ethnic minorities. Chinese culture took a severe beating during the Cultural Revolution; the older generations carry many scars from the past and their way of thinking is often in complete opposition to the worldliness and fearlessness of younger Beijingers. While Beijing is a modern metropolis, traditional ideas and ways continue to seep into the lifestyles of many of its residents.

Religion

In recent years, Beijingers have been returning to restored temples with armfuls of incense to appease their gods and ancestors. The dominating religions of Confucianism, Taoism and Buddhism have influenced each other and society for centuries.

Buddhism and Taoism give reverence to gods and goddesses who preside over earth and the afterlife. Confucianism is more a philosophy than a religion, dealing with the affairs of life but not death. Confucianism defines codes of conduct and a patriarchal pattern of obedience; respect flows upwards from child to adult, woman to man and subject to ruler. Not surprisingly, it was adopted by the state for two millennia.

These days, the government is nondenominational and is not overly concerned with religious groups unless they are believed to challenge state doctrine, as was the case with the quasi-Buddhist exercise regime Falun Gong, whose thousands of practitioners have been menaced into obscurity.

Feng Shui

Literally meaning 'wind and water', feng shui is a collection of ancient geomantic principles that see bodies of water and landforms directing the cosmic currents of the universal *qi* (energy). To follow feng shui guidelines is to create a positive path for *qi*, which can maximise a person's wealth, happiness, longevity and fertility. Ignoring the principles and blocking the

> **Face Value**
> Loosely defined as status, ego or self-respect, the concept of face is not unfamiliar to most foreigners. Essentially it's about avoiding being made to look stupid or wrong. What you may find unfamiliar is the lengths Chinese people will go to in order to save face. If a conflict arises, opponents dig in their heels; screaming matches on the streets or in shops are not uncommon. Chinese people will assume that you also want to save face and will hand over one of their ready-to-wear excuses should they feel you need it. Try never to accuse someone directly; unless you love to argue, outright confrontation should be reserved as a last resort.

flow can spell disaster. Temples, tombs, houses and even whole cities have been built in feng shui fashion to harmonise with the surrounding landscape. Within a building, the order of rooms and arrangement of furniture can also inhibit or enhance *qi* flow. The barging through of railways and roads and the construction of high-rises has incensed some residents, who believe the balance of the geography is being disturbed.

Family

Family has traditionally been the smallest unit in Chinese society and the more recent emergence of the individual has challenged its values. The traditional Chinese family is interdependent; younger generations depend on older generations for wisdom and guidance, and older generations depend on the young for subsistence and care. China's One-Child Policy (see p39) is changing the shape of families, creating a 4-2-1 balance (four grandparents, two parents and one child); if traditional values and practices survive, today's children will each potentially have six elderly dependents.

Etiquette

Many frustrations experienced by foreigners in China are based on cultural misunderstandings; what might be considered rude in the West may well be normal behaviour in China. For example, you queue for a subway ticket only to have customer after customer barge in front of you. After finally getting onto the train, someone practically sits on top of you. You glare at them only to be met with a grin. Keep your cool. In China, where queues are unheard of and privacy exists in the mind and not in the space around you, this is normal, not rude.

> ### Strings Attached
> *Guanxi*, or connections, string together much of Chinese society; you're either in the loop or you're not. It's the old practice of 'you scratch my back and I'll scratch yours'. In business it's referred to as 'going through the back door' and it can lead to anything from tickets on an oversold train to a job you have no qualifications for. When you meet Chinese people, the conversation may turn to what you've got to offer and how they can help you – they're throwing you the *guanxi* line.

There are, however, a few things that are considered rude. When given a business card or piece of paper, always receive it with both hands. When writing something, use any colour ink but red, as it denotes unfriendliness. When giving gifts, money is insulting but imported goods carry much prestige and will win you points. You can smoke when you like but always offer the pack (not single cigarettes) around first.

ARTS
Acrobatics

Chinese acrobatic troupes will blow you away. Young contortionists turn themselves inside out and upside down while platespinners whiz countless plates through the air. Circus acts have a long history in China, dating back 2000 years. Routines were developed using simple everyday objects like sticks, hoops, chairs and jars. Today, many of the acts in Beijing keep the traditional routines alive while others incorporate modern props like roller blades. Difficult acts to follow include 'Peacock Displaying its Feathers' (a dozen or more people balanced on one bicycle) and 'Pagoda of Bowls' (a performer does everything with her torso except tie it in knots, while balancing a stack of bowls on her foot, head, or both).

> ### Cut it out!
> For over 1500 years, scissors and knives have been wielded to cut paper into intricate images. Traditionally, papercuttings have been burned at temples for gods and ancestors. As folk art, it was used to judge would-be brides and to develop patterns for embroidery and lacquer work. Today, papercuttings are primarily produced for decoration and you will see them hung on walls, doors and lanterns. Each Chinese New Year, most residents replace last year's papercuttings on doors and entrances with freshly cut symbols of luck and fortune.

Martial Arts

Martial arts combine discipline, flexibility, spirituality and defence. Practised in China for centuries, three of the most common forms are taijiquan (usually called taiji or t'ai chi), gongfu (kung fu) and qigong. In all forms, respect and responsibility are considered paramount, while fighting is seen as a last resort. T'ai chi is very slow and fluid and its motions mirror everyday actions like gathering water. Gongfu has become popular through Hong Kong films, and focuses on self-defence. Qigong is a form of energy management aimed at maintaining good mental and physical health. Qigong masters have been known to project their *qi* in miraculous ways – from healing others to driving nails through boards with their bare fingers.

Music

Musical instruments have been unearthed from Shang-dynasty tombs, and Chinese folk songs can be traced back at least this far. Today, traditional musical concerts are on the boom in Beijing. Performances feature the *sheng* (flute), *erhu* (two-stringed fiddle), *huqin* (viola), *yueqin* (guitar), *guzheng* (zither), *pipa* (lute) and the ceremonial *suona* (trumpet). These instruments are also the musical stars of Chinese opera.

China has a thriving contemporary-music scene. Largely initiated by Cui Jian, Beijing's face of rock, punk bands like Underground Baby and metal groups like Tang Dynasty have gained Beijing the reputation as China's rock-music Mecca. DJ culture has also arrived in Beijing in a big way.

Opera

Beijing opera is China's most famous form of theatre. With a history of some 900 years, the opera stage has brought together disparate art forms like acrobatics, martial arts, poetic arias and stylised dance. Traditionally, opera performers were male only and at the very bottom of the social ladder, on a par with prostitutes and slaves. Despite this, opera remained a popular form of entertainment, included in festivals, marriages and even funerals. Most performances were open-air, compelling performers to develop a piercing style of singing that could be heard above the crowds, and to wear garish costumes that could be seen through the poor lighting of oil lamps. Performances continue to be loud and bright, with singers taking on stylised roles instantly recognised by the audience. The four major roles are the female role, the male role, the 'painted-face' role (for gods and warriors) and the clown.

Painting

A traditional Chinese painting may be achieved in a very short time, but only following much thought and total conception of the piece in the artist's mind beforehand. The brush line, which varies in thickness and tone, is the important feature; shading is regarded as a foreign

Exhibits from Wang Yuping's 'Peephole series' at the Red Gate Gallery

technique and colour plays only a minor symbolic and decorative role. Figure painting dominated the scene from the Han dynasty (206BC-AD220) until Taoist painters began landscape painting in the 4th and 5th centuries.

It wasn't until the 20th century that there was any real departure from tradition. In the early days of Communism, artistic talent was used to glorify the revolution. These days you'll find a flourishing avant-garde art scene in Beijing, with young artists gaining critical acclaim worldwide.

Literature

Over time, Beijing has both produced and attracted well-known authors. Lao She, a novelist of the early 20th century, penned numerous novels in the capital, including *Rickshaw Boy*, a social critique of the living conditions of rickshaw drivers in Beijing. Other writers who resided in Beijing include Lu Xun, Mao Dun and Guo Moruo.

When the Communists came to power, writing became a hazardous occupation and many writers did not survive. These days, the situation has improved somewhat; writers continue to skirt around politically taboo issues but do explore social realities. Author Zhang Jie has been labelled China's first feminist writer for her internationally acclaimed *Love Must Not Be Forgotten,* while Wang Shuo's short stories express the realities of Beijing's growing subclass of unemployed and disaffected youth.

Directory

Soldier on guard in front of the Gate of Heavenly Peace

ARRIVAL & DEPARTURE

Direct flights from Europe, the Americas and Asia vie for touchdown at Capital International Airport. Competition within the airline industry means good deals are available, particularly in the low season (Oct-May). Trains chug in from Russia along the Trans-Siberian Railway or you can take a longwinded train journey from Hong Kong or Vietnam. You can also get pretty close to Beijing by sea from South Korea or Japan to Tianjin.

Air

Beijing's flashy Capital International Airport is 27km northeast of the city centre. Domestic and international terminals are next door to one another. Hotel shuttles, buses and taxis transport passengers into town via the Shoudujichang Expressway.

LEFT LUGGAGE

Left-luggage facilities are on the ground floor of the international terminal. Luggage can be stored for up to seven days. You'll be charged according to the size of your bag.

INFORMATION

General Inquiries	☎	6456 3604
Flight Information		
Air Canada	☎	6468 2001
Air France	☎	6588 1388
American Airlines	☎	6517 1788
British Airways	☎	6512 4070
Japan Airlines	☎	6513 0888
Korean Air	☎	6505 0088
Lufthansa Airlines	☎	6465 4488
Qantas Airways	☎	6467 4794
Singapore Airlines	☎	6505 2233

Hotel Booking Service
The information desk at the international arrivals hall has a hotel booking service. You pay a deposit here and the hotel returns it to you upon your arrival.

AIRPORT ACCESS

Bus There is a bewildering choice of buses into town. Inside the terminal there's a service desk where you can buy tickets; explain where you want to go, hand over your Y16 and you should be directed to the right bus. Bus journeys into Beijing take anywhere from half an hour to an hour and head to points all over the city.

Three of the buses follow express routes into town. Route A is the most popular; it passes by the Youyi Lufthansa Centre, Dongzhimen and Dongsishitiao subway stops and terminates downtown at the International Youth Hostel.

Returning to the airport, you can catch a shuttle from Xidan subway station, outside the Civil Aviation Administration of China (CAAC) booking office.

Shuttle Many hotels run shuttles between the airport and their front door; ask about it when you book.

Taxi Getting a taxi into town is fairly economical (about Y85 including the Y15 expressway toll) and only takes around 20mins if you don't get caught in a traffic jam. There are a number of dodgy taxi operators who will attempt to lure you into a Y300 ride while you are still in the terminal. Ignore them, head out to the taxi queue and find a driver willing to use the meter.

Train

Domestic trains arrive and depart at Beijing Train Station (4, J11) or Beijing West Train Station (3, H6). Tibet is the only Chinese province not covered by the country's extensive rail network. International trains for Moscow, Pyongyang and Ulaan Baatar arrive and depart from Beijing Train Station, while trains for Hong Kong and Vietnam use Beijing West Train Station.

Domestic train tickets (hard seat, soft seat or sleeper) can be bought up to four days in advance, which includes the day you buy the ticket and the day you depart. You can scrum for them at the station or get them at most hotels for a small surcharge. Do your best to avoid travelling during holidays, particularly Chinese New Year, when tickets are rare and trains are congested.

Tickets for the Trans-Siberian, Trans-Manchurian and Trans-Mongolian Railways can be purchased at Monkey Business (4, D14; ☎ 6591 6519), which is located above the Hidden Tree, or through the Beijing Tourism Group (7th fl, 28 Jianguomen Wai Dajie; 4, H12; ☎ 6515 8562, 6515 8844 for tickets). Note that visas can be quite complicated for these trips.

Boat

While Beijing isn't on the coast, the seaport of Tianjin (2½hrs away) has weekly boats to and from Kobe in Japan and twice-weekly boats to Incheon in South Korea. Tickets can be bought in Tianjin from the shipping office (☎ 022-2331 2283) or at the port (☎ 022-2938 3961).

Travel Documents
PASSPORT

All visitors to Beijing require a visa and therefore a passport. Passports must be valid for at least three months longer than the expiry date of the visa.

VISA

Nationals of all countries require a visa to visit China (with the exception of those from Hong Kong and Macau). Visas must be arranged at embassies or consulates before arriving in China; they take about three days to process if you apply in person and are valid for one to three months.

The 'valid until' date on the visa is the date by which you must enter the country, not the date upon which your visa expires. Information and printable visa application forms can be found at 🖳 www.china-embassy.org.

RETURN/ONWARD TICKET

You may need to show your return ticket when applying for your visa.

Customs

As a tourist, customs officers are unlikely to pay you much attention. You can only legally carry Y6000 across the border and while there is no restriction on foreign currency, you should declare amounts exceeding US$5000. If you're trying to take out anything considered an antique (ie made before 1949), you'll require a certificate and a red seal, obtainable from the Relics Bureau (4, H13; Friendship Store; ☎ 6401 4608; Mon-Fri 1.30-4.30pm). It is illegal to take home antique objects from Tibet or antiques made before 1795.

Departure Tax

If you're departing by air, a Y90 departure tax is levied for each passenger. This can only be paid in cash; if you don't have enough, visit one of the ATMs or exchange desks at the airport. You must pay departure tax before going through security. Nobody checks until you get all the way to customs and if you don't have your receipt you'll be sent back.

GETTING AROUND

Train

The subway is your best option for getting around town; delays are rare and it only gets seriously crowded during the 5pm rush hour. Trains run every few minutes from 5am-11pm. With a Y3 ticket you can travel any distance and switch lines. At the moment, there are only two lines; however, the city is ambitiously planning for five more to be opened before the 2008 Olympics.

To spot a subway station, look for the blue capital 'D' with a circle around it. Platform signs are in Chinese and Pinyin. Unfortunately, the subway is not accessible for disabled travellers. If you visit northern Beijing you may also encounter a new light train that winds its way through the suburbs.

Bus

While you'll see countless public buses plying the streets, they are generally a frustrating way of getting around. The tangle of routes can be bewildering to short-stay travellers and traffic can slow buses to an infuriating crawl. Bus maps can be handy but are also fairly cryptic, with numbers disappearing at one end of town and reappearing at the other. Buses run from 5am to 11pm and tickets cost around Y1. At almost any time of day, buses can be packed to the gills; your chances of getting a seat are just about nil.

Buses displaying one- and two-digit route numbers operate in the city centre. Buses displaying three-digit numbers beginning with one (eg 102) are trolley, those with three-digit numbers beginning with two are night buses and those beginning with three are part of the suburban line. Private minibuses follow many of the main bus routes; they're slightly more expensive than city buses and can be slower and more dangerous. Double-decker buses do loops around the city centre and are much less traumatic. A ticket costs Y2 and you are almost guaranteed a seat.

Taxi

Unless there's a rainstorm or it's rush hour, you should have no problem hailing a taxi. If you don't speak Chinese, try to have your destination written down in Chinese characters.

As in any big city, taxi drivers may attempt to take you on a wild goose chase; hold onto a map and look like you know where you're going. Most Beijing taxi drivers are fair and efficient; in the unlikely event that they don't want to use the meter, insist that they do or get out. Don't expect rear seatbelts in any but the best taxis, and watch out for exhausted drivers.

Every taxi has a red sticker on the side rear window showing its rate per kilometre. Red Xiali (the make of the car) are the most economical (Y10/4km, then Y1.2/km). Next are Citroens, which have more legroom, and then Volkswagen Sanatans (prices vary). Between 11pm and 6am there's a 20% surcharge added to the flag-fall metered fare.

You can rent a cab for the hour or the day (minimum Y350). For phone bookings call Beijing Taxi (☎ 6837 3399) or Capital Taxi (☎ 6487 2387).

Bicycle

Beijing by bike can be fantastic fun. The city is fairly flat and there are lots of bike lanes. Major thoroughfares are best avoided, as thick traffic and bad drivers can make them extremely dangerous. *Hutongs* (alleyways) are best explored on bike.

You can rent bikes at hotels or rental shops. Theft can be a problem in Beijing; lock your bike and park it in a patrolled bike parking lot. Few bikes are equipped with lights and helmets are nowhere to be seen.

Car

If you're a confident driver and are willing to brave Beijing's mad traffic, you can hire a car. However, given the restrictions and the recklessness you'll see on the roads, it can hardly be recommended. Rather than do the driving yourself, it's much less hassle to hire a chauffeur-driven car.

ROAD RULES

You will quickly begin to wonder if there are any. Not even the lanes appear to mean much; the most consistent rule seems to be carelessness. The majority of cars drive on the right, as required by law, and seat belts are compulsory for front-seat passengers. Speed limits are posted. While you don't see many road checks for drinking and driving, tolerance is zilch.

RENTAL

One of the best (and only) places to hire a car is the Hertz Office (☎ 0 106 444 2375; 🖳 www .hertz.net.cn) at the airport. Prices start from Y400/day and there's a Y8000 deposit. Beijing Car Solutions (Jia Li Hotel, 21 Jiang Tai Lu, Chaoyang; ☎ 1 350 138 0047;

🖥 www.car-solution.com) offers car rental and assistance. Chauffeur-driven cars can be arranged at major hotels and travel agencies. Depending on the type of vehicle, it can cost as much as Y1000/day. You're better off hiring a Xiali taxi for the day.

DRIVING LICENCE & PERMIT

You will require an International Driving Licence if you plan to drive in Beijing. Even with this licence, you're only allowed to drive within Beijing and Tianjin proper and cannot set out further afield.

PRACTICALITIES

Climate & When to Go

Autumn (mid-Sept–Nov) sees gorgeous weather, with blue skies and manageable temperatures. This is the best time to visit Beijing. More and more foreign tourists are catching on to this and it's becoming increasingly busy (and expensive) in top-end hotels.

Summer runs from June to mid-September and can be absolutely scorching and humid, making sightseeing a sweaty affair. This is the high season for Chinese tourists; sights are often packed out and the Great Wall nearly collapses under the weight of marching feet.

Spring (Apr–May) is quiet, but the worsening sand storms that sweep in from Inner Mongolia can be blinding, to say the least. Winter (Dec–Mar) brings the best deals, when hotels and places of interest drop their rates for the occasional tourists; it's also glacial outside.

Tourist Information
TOURIST INFORMATION ABROAD

China International Travel Services (CITS), a state-run travel agency, has offices in major cities around the globe. Unfortunately, their services are usually inefficient and fairly limited. Their brochures might be great propaganda but they're not very useful. Representatives include:

Australia (☎ 02-9299 4057; fax 9290 1958; 🖥 citsaust@travman.com.au; 19th fl, 44 Market St, Sydney, NSW 2000)

Canada (☎ 416-599 6636; fax 416-599 6382; 🖥 cits@citscanada.com; Suite 806, 480 University Ave, Toronto, ON M5G 1V2)

France (☎ 01 56 59 10 10; fax 01 53 75 32 88; Office du Tourisme de Chine, 15 rue de Berri, 75008 Paris)

Hong Kong (☎ 2732 5888; fax 2721 7154; 12th fl, Tower A, New Mandarin Plaza, 14 Science Museum Rd, Tsimshatsui East)

UK (☎ 020-7935 9787; fax 7487 5842; 4 Glentworth St, London NW1)

USA CA (☎ 818-545 7505; fax 545 7506; 🖥 citslax@aol.com; Suite 201, 333 W Broadway, Glendale, CA 91204) NY (☎ 212-760 8218; fax 760 8809; 🖥 citsusany@aol.com; Suite 6413, Empire State Bldg, 350 Fifth Ave, New York, NY 10118)

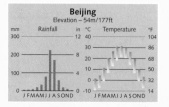

Beijing
Elevation – 54m/177ft

LOCAL TOURIST INFORMATION

Chinese tourist offices seem to be more of a business than a public service. They have information on their own tours but anything else seems beyond them. If you're looking for specific information about Beijing, you're better off asking the concierge at your hotel. The Tourist Information Centre (10 Dengshikou Xijie; 4, F8; ☎ 6512 3043; 9am-6pm) is somewhat more helpful (though most staff are not very confident in English) and you can get free tourist maps here.

You can book tours and train and plane tickets at the Beijing Tourism Group (7th fl, 28 Jianguomen Wai Dajie; 4, H12; ☎ 6515 8562; fax 6515 8603) as well as glean limited information about the city.

China International Travel Service (ground fl, 9 Jianguomen Nei Dajie; 4, H11; CITS; 🖳 www .citsbj.com) isn't particularly forthcoming with information, but is more than happy to book you on one of its many city tours. There is also the English-language 24hr Beijing Tourism Hotline (☎ 6513 0828) that can answer questions and listen to complaints.

Embassies

Embassies in Beijing:
Australia (4, B14; ☎ 6532 2331; fax 6532 6957; 🖳 www.austemb.org.cn; 21 Dongzhimen Wai Dajie)
Canada (4, B14; ☎ 6532 4846; fax 6532 4072; 🖳 www.canada.org .cn/beijing; 19 Dongzhimen Wai Dajie)
France (4, C15; ☎ 6532 1331; fax 6532 4737; 🖳 www.ambafrance-cn.org; 3 Dongsan Jie)

New Zealand (4, G14; ☎ 6532 2731; fax 6532 4317; 🖳 www.nzembassy .com/china; 1 Ritan Dong Erjie)
Russia (4, A11; ☎ 6532 2051; fax 6532 4851; 4 Dongzhimen Beizhongjie)
Thailand (4, G12; ☎ 6532 1749; fax 6532 1748; 40 Guanghua Lu)
UK (4, G14; ☎ 6532 1961; fax 6532 1937; 🖳 www.britishembassy.org.cn; 11 Guanghua Lu)
USA (4, G14; ☎ 6532 3831; fax 6532 3431; 🖳 www.usembassy-china .org.cn; 3 Xiushui Beijie)

Money
CURRENCY

Chinese currency is called Renminbi (RMB) or 'people's money'. Its basic unit is the yuan (Y), also referred to as kuai, the equivalent slang to buck or quid. The yuan is divided into 10 jiao (pronounced mao) and the jiao is divided into 10 fen.

These days, fen are worth next to nothing and are disappearing from use. Paper notes are issued in denominations of one, two, five, 10, 20, 50 and 100 yuan; one, two and five jiao; and one, two and five fen. Coins are in denominations of one yuan; one, two and five jiao; and one, two and five fen.

Beijing is flooded with counterfeit money and many shops will try to flog it to foreigners. Fake notes are usually in Y100 or Y50 denominations; try to keep smaller notes for shopping and check your change carefully. Counterfeit notes are often really poor renditions and obvious even to the untrained eye.

TRAVELLERS CHEQUES

Besides the advantage of security, travellers cheques are good to carry in China as they offer a more favourable exchange rate than cash; the only drawback is that they can be a pain to cash. Technically, cheques from most of the world's leading banks and issuing agencies are accepted in Beijing, the most obvious being Citibank, American Express and Visa.

You can exchange cheques at the main branch of the Bank of China (Oriental Plaza; 4, H9), exchange desks at the airport, occasionally at China International Trust & Investment Corporation (CITIC) Banks and at some of the larger tourist hotels. Banks give the official rate, as do most hotels (hotels also add a commission charge). The Friendship Store and major department stores also exchange travellers cheques for a commission, but no-one accepts them as hard currency.

CREDIT CARDS

Most four- and five-star hotels, fancy restaurants and major department stores accept credit cards. If you use your credit card for a cash advance at the Bank of China or CITIC Bank you will be levied with a steep 4% commission. For 24hr assistance call:

American Express	☎ 6505 2888
Diners Club	☎ 6510 1833
24hr hotline	☎ 6606 2227
MasterCard	☎ 10 800 110 7309
Visa	☎ 10 800 110 2911

ATMS

A growing number of ATMs are springing up in Beijing. Cards with GlobalAccess, Cirrus, Interlink, Plus and Star are all commonly accepted. You can also get cash advances on Visa, MasterCard and Amex at many ATMs. The maximum withdrawal for all bankcards is Y2500/day. It's always good to have a backup and not depend solely on your bankcard, as ATMs are often out of service or out of money.

Bank of China ATMs can be found at Capital Airport, Wangfujing Dajie, Swissotel (4, C12), Palace Hotel (4, F9) and the Youyi Lufthansa Centre (3, D13). The Hong Kong and Shanghai Banking Corporation have a 24hr ATM in the COFCO Plaza (8 Jianguomen Dajie; 4, H11), where you can withdraw money from your overseas HSBC account.

CHANGING MONEY

Foreign currency can be exchanged at the Bank of China, exchange desks at the airport, CITIC Bank and tourist hotels. Banks give the official rate as do most hotels, though many hotels add a small commission and some will only exchange money for their own guests.

Hold onto at least a few of your exchange receipts as, theoretically, you'll need them if you want to exchange any remaining RMB at the end of your trip.

Most banks are open Mon-Fri from 8.30am to 5pm or 6pm. Many close for an hour at lunch time and some are open Saturday mornings.

Tipping

It is not customary to tip in Beijing, however, foreigners are slowly introducing the idea. Most top-end hotels and many of the city's classier restaurants will add a

10% to 15% service charge. You don't need to add an additional tip unless the service is exemplary and you feel moved to do so. Porters are the notable exception and will expect a small tip.

Discounts

Whether or not you qualify for a child's ticket is generally determined by your height rather than your age. Kids under 1.2m often get into sights for half-price, as do students and seniors with recognised ID.

The Beijing Museum Ticket is valid for one year and will get you into around 60 museums for Y80. You can purchase the ticket at participating museums or at the Wangfujing train station.

STUDENT & YOUTH CARDS

Students with ISIC or STA cards receive discounts at many of Beijing's major sights. Unfortunately, discounts don't extend to travel.

SENIORS' CARDS

Discounts for seniors are often given but not listed at attractions. Show some ID that has your date of birth – you may be pleasantly surprised.

Opening Hours

Businesses are generally open Mon-Fri from 8.30am or 9am to 5pm or 6pm. Most close for an hour over lunch and many are open on Saturday morning. Shops are often open on Saturday and Sunday. While many shops don't open until 10am, they stay open until 10pm seven days a week.

Restaurants are usually open between 11am-2pm and 6-10pm. Most sights are open from 9am to 4.30pm or 5pm; almost all are open over the weekend and a few are closed on Monday. Almost all parks are open daily from 6am-9pm.

Public Holidays

1 Jan	New Year's Day
Late Jan/ early Feb	Chinese New Year (3 days)
8 Mar	International Women's Day
1 May	International Labour Day
4 May	Youth Day
1 June	Children's Day
1 Jul	Anniversary of the Founding of the Chinese Communist Party
1 Aug	Anniversary of the Founding of the People's Liberation Army
1 Oct	National Day

Time

Despite covering numerous world time zones, all of China is on Beijing Standard Time, which is eight hours ahead of GMT/UTC. At noon in Beijing it's:

11pm the previous day in New York
8pm the previous day in Los Angeles
4am in London
5am in Paris
4pm in Wellington
2pm in Melbourne and Sydney

Electricity

Beijing's electric current is 220V, 50Hz AC. Most plugs will take four designs: three-pronged angled pins (as in Australia), three-pronged round pins (as in Hong Kong), two flat pins (US style, without the ground wire) and two narrow

116 | **DIRECTORY**

round pins (European style). You should be able to run your laptop without a problem. Conversion plugs are widely available in Beijing.

Weights & Measures

China officially uses the international metric system. See the conversion table below. If you buy food from street vendors, you'll likely encounter China's ancient weights and measures system of *liang* and *jin*. One *jin* is 0.6kg (1.32lbs) or about three bananas, and one *liang* is 37.5g (1.32oz); there are 16 *liang* to the *jin*.

TEMPERATURE
°C = (°F - 32) ÷ 1.8
°F = (°C x 1.8) + 32

DISTANCE
1in = 2.54cm
1cm = 0.39in
1m = 3.3ft = 1.1yd
1ft = 0.3m
1km = 0.62 miles
1 mile = 1.6km

WEIGHT
1kg = 2.2lb
1lb = 0.45kg
1g = 0.04oz
1oz = 28g

VOLUME
1L = 0.26 US gallons
1 US gallon = 3.8L
1L = 0.22 imperial gallons
1 imperial gallon = 4.55L

Post

China Post is fairly reliable and your postcards and parcels should make it overseas in good time. You can buy stamps at any post office, the most efficient being Beijing Main Post Office (Jianguomen Beidajie; 4, G12; Mon-Sat 8am-7pm). You can also send parcels from here, but don't seal them up before you have them inspected by the postal staff. For anything considered an antique, you'll need the correct paperwork (see Customs p110). Smaller post offices are generally open Mon-Fri 8.30am-5pm and Sat 8.30am-noon.

Other convenient post offices can be found in the CITIC Building (4, H13) and in the basement of the China World Trade Centre (4, H15). You can also post your letters via the reception desk at your hotel.

POSTAL RATES

Postage for airmail letters (up to 20g) sent to anywhere outside China costs Y4.40, postcards cost Y3.20 and aerogrammes Y5.20. It costs Y123 to airmail a parcel weighing 1-2kg.

Telephone

International and domestic calls can be made easily from your hotel room. Local calls from your hotel room are free. From orange public pay phones or domestic phones at kiosks, you can make local calls for around two jiao. Long-distance international calls can also be made from orange phone booths, but they're pricey (Y15/min to the USA or Europe). Between midnight and 7am calls are 40% cheaper. You can also make international calls from main telecommunications offices.

PHONECARDS

There are a wide range of local and international phonecards available. The best deal is Internet Phone (IP); rates are Y2.40/min to North America, Y1.50 to Hong Kong, Macau or Taiwan and Y3.20 to all other countries. IP cards come in denominations of Y100 and can be purchased at most hotels and kiosks.

Lonely Planet's ekno Communication Card, specifically aimed at travellers, provides competitive international call rates (avoid using it for local calls), messaging services and free email. Log on to ☐ www.ekno.lonelyplanet.com for details on joining and accessing the service.

MOBILE PHONES

Check if your mobile phone has a setting for use in China. Beijing's mobile-phone shops can sell you a phone and a number for around Y200; you then buy credit for calls. You can often rent mobiles for a short period of time from business centres in top-end hotels.

COUNTRY & CITY CODES

People's Republic of China	☎ 86
Beijing	☎ 010

USEFUL PHONE NUMBERS

Note that there is a 50% chance that the people at the other end of these lines do not speak English.

Local Directory Inquiries	☎ 114
International Directory Inquiries	☎ 115
Time	☎ 117
Weather	☎ 121

INTERNATIONAL DIRECT DIAL CODES

Dial ☎ 00 followed by:

Australia	☎ 61
Canada	☎ 1
Japan	☎ 81
New Zealand	☎ 64
UK	☎ 44
USA	☎ 1

Digital Resources

Lonely Planet website (☐ www.lonelyplanet.com) offers a speedy link to many of Beijing's websites. Others to try include:

The Beijing Page (☐ www.beijingpage.com)

Beijing Tourism Administration (☐ www.bjta.gov.cn)

China Business World (☐ www.cbw.com/tourism)

China Now (☐ www.chinanow.com)

China Online (☐ www.chinaonline.com)

Fly China (☐ www.flychina.com)

Muzi (☐ www.muzi.net)

Webtix (☐ www.webtix.com.cn)

Wild China (☐ www.wildchina.com)

Doing Business

Doing business in China takes patience. Obtaining licences, hiring employees and paying taxes can generate mind-boggling quantities of red tape. It's a 'who you know' system and it can take a lot of persistence to find a cooperative official. Hopefully, with China joining the World Trade Organization (WTO), it will become less of a minefield.

The trade section of your embassy in Beijing may be able to get you started, as can one of the many Trade Promotion Organisations like the American Chamber of Commerce (☎ 8519 1920; ☐ www.amcham-china.org.cn), the China Council for the Promotion of International Trade (☎ 6801 3344; ☐ www.ccpit.org) or the British Chamber of Commerce (☎ 6593 2150; ☐ www.britaininchina.com). Also try to get your hands on a copy of *Business Beijing*, a monthly magazine available in many hotel lobbies.

For help with accounting, try Price Waterhouse (☎ 6606 1155; fax 8529 9000), for lawyers call Denton, Wilde & Sapte (☎ 6505 4891; fax 6505 4893) and for printing, head to Kinko's (Dongsanhuan Beilu; 4, D15; ☎ 6595 8020; fax 6595 8218; 🖳 Beijing01@kinkos.com.cn; 24hrs).

Business centres in major hotels can provide office equipment, secretarial assistance, conference rooms and translation services. You can also try Translations Sinofile (☎ 6605 9198; 🖳 sinofile@sinofile.com) for translations, and Phone Rent (☎ 6586 6665; 🖳 www.phonerent.com) or Plaza Business Centre (Kerry Centre; 4, G15; ☎ 8529 8000; 🖳 www.pbc-asia.com) for office equipment, meeting rooms, translators and interpreters.

Newspapers & Magazines

The Chinese government's favourite English-language mouthpiece is the *China Daily* (🖳 www.chinadaily.net), which you can pick up for free in hotel lobbies or buy for Y1. Magazines and newspapers from North America and Europe are available in major tourist hotels and the Friendship Store. Look for *Time*, *Newsweek*, *The Economist*, the *Asian Wall Street Journal*, *The Financial Times* and the *International Herald Tribune*. These papers are sometimes trimmed of opinion; for the uncensored version visit the newspapers' websites.

Beijing also has a plethora of English-language listings magazines available free at most tourist hotels and from Sanlitun bars and restaurants. *That's Beijing* is the best of the bunch.

Television

Channel CCTV9 is Beijing's English-language channel, offering painfully dull drivel and propaganda news. CCTV4 occasionally carries more interesting English-language programs on travel in China, and CCTV5 has sports in Chinese. Many tourist hotels have ESPN, CNN and HBO.

Photography & Video

Colour-print film, including Kodak and Fuji, is readily available, as are lithium camera batteries. Colour-slide film can be found in many camera shops and one-hour processing is becoming common. Kodak shops are on every other corner, although some are better at developing film than others. Try Gold One Photo Services (14 Xinyuan Jie; 4, A15; ☎ 6468 6895; 8.30am-10.30pm).

China subscribes to the PAL video standard, the same as Australia, New Zealand, the UK and most of Europe. DVDs and VCDs are more widely used in China than videotapes.

Health
IMMUNISATIONS

No vaccination requirements exist for entry into China, except for yellow fever if you are coming from an infected area. As a basic precaution, check that your tetanus, diphtheria and polio vaccinations are up to date. Vaccinations against hepatitis A and B are also worth considering, as is one against influenza, particularly for senior travellers. Malaria is not a risk in Beijing.

PRECAUTIONS

Other than the thick layer of smog that sometimes blankets the city, Beijing is a relatively healthy place. Influenza is almost synonymous with China and there have been outbreaks of nasty viruses, Severe Acute Respiratory Syndrome (SARS) being a notorious example.

An illness that travellers are prone to is diarrhoea, brought on by ingesting food and water that are foreign to your body. It's best to drink bottled water (make sure bottles are sealed when you buy them) and peel all fruit and vegetables. Avoid eating raw vegetables in all but the most foreigner-friendly restaurants. The extreme weather conditions can also play havoc with your system, and heatstroke can bring on a case of the runs.

Travellers after current health advisories for China should check the World Health Organization website 🖥 www.who.int.

INSURANCE & MEDICAL TREATMENT

Travel insurance is advisable to cover any medical treatment you may need while in Beijing. Services that cater to foreigners have English-speaking staff and offer a high, international standard of care. It's often much cheaper to ask which medicines you need and then purchase them at a pharmacy rather than at the hospital.

MEDICAL SERVICES

Hospitals with 24hr accident and emergency departments include:

Beijing International Medical Centre (3, D13; ☎ 6465 1561/2/3; Room S106-S111, Youyi Lufthansa Centre, 50 Liangmaqiao Lu; Ⓜ Dongzhimen)
Beijing International SOS Clinic (4, B14; ☎ 6462 9112, 24hr emergency centre ☎ 6462 9100; 1 Xinfu Sancun Beijie; Ⓜ Dongzhimen)
Beijing Union Hospital (4, G9; ☎ 6529 5284, emergency ☎ 6529 5269; 53 Dongdan Beidajie; Ⓜ Dongdan)
The Hong Kong International Medical Clinic (4, C12; ☎ 6501 2288 ext 2345/6; 9th fl, Hong Kong Macau Centre, Swissotel, Gongren Tiyuchang Beilu; Ⓜ Dongsishitiao)

DENTAL SERVICES

If you chip a tooth or require emergency treatment, head to the Beijing International Medical Centre or the Hong Kong International Medical Clinic (see above).

PHARMACIES

Pharmacies are everywhere and they usually sell both traditional and Western medicines. It's easy to buy drugs that you would normally require a prescription for at home – make sure you know what you're taking. Try the following places:

Beijing Wanweierkang Dayaodian (4, G9; ☎ 6559 5763; 62 Dongdan Beijdajie)
Golden Elephant Pharmacy (4, H3; ☎ 6602 0885/0730; 24hrs; 114 Xidan Beidajie)

Wangfujing Medicine Shop (4, G8; ☎ 6524 0122; 8.30am-9pm; 267 Wangfujing Dajie)

Toilets

Despite the proud claim of having invented the first flushing toilet, China's loos can be a heinous assault on the senses. Be pleased to know that Beijing's toilets are pristine compared to those in China's countryside. In most tourist hotels you'll find Western-style toilets; at sights and restaurants, you'll find squat-style toilets in a variety of conditions.

Places like McDonald's and major tourist sights usually have clean toilets. If you're down a *hutong* and need the loo, you'll experience truly public toilets. Located every block or so, these are what the locals use – to find them just follow your nose. Toilet paper is not often available, so carry some with you.

You may have to pay to use a toilet so keep some change handy. Also, Beijing's sewerage system can't handle toilet paper; just drop it in the basket beside the toilet. For toilet ratings, fees, cleanliness, style and a good laugh, check out 'The Bathroom Diaries' at 🖵 www.bathroomdiaries.com/china/beijing.html.

Safety Concerns

The consequence for crime against foreigners is steep in China (often death), so you are generally very safe and given little attention by criminals. Nevertheless, as with any large city, Beijing has its fair share of minor theft such as pickpocketing; many feel this is on the rise, with increased unemployment in the city.

In crowded places like buses or markets, carry your bag in front of you and keep some small change in your pocket to avoid opening up your wallet. Pickpockets tend to slice open bags and pockets with razors. A money belt is the safest way to carry things. Don't walk alone along empty streets at night and don't wander off by yourself into deserted areas of parks.

Hotels are usually safe places to leave things, as each floor has an attendant. Even so, don't leave your passport and valuables lying around; if you don't have a safe in your room, check if there's one at reception. Dormitories are less safe, with the added risk of other travellers making off with your things.

You'll encounter beggars around temples and in neighbourhoods frequented by foreigners. They're often mothers or children, many of whom can become aggressive; they're desperate but they're not known to be harmful.

You may be approached by art students who will invite you to an art exhibition they're having nearby. While some people who go along enjoy meeting the students and buy a painting or two, most people come away feeling bullied into buying something and seriously ripped off.

Spitting may not seem like an unlikely safety concern but just wait until you experience it. Technically, spitting is illegal in Beijing, but many locals continue to gob with gusto. Do your best to keep out of the line of fire.

KEEPING COPIES
Make photocopies of all your important documents. Keep some with you, separate from the originals, and leave a copy at home. You can also store details of documents in Lonely Planet's free online Travel Vault; see 🖳 www .ekno.lonelyplanet.com for details.

Emergency Numbers
Ambulance ☎ 120
Fire ☎ 119
General Emergency ☎ 999
Police ☎ 110

Women Travellers
Principles of decorum and respect for women are deeply ingrained in Chinese culture. Chinese males are not macho and there is a strong sense of balance between the sexes. Much of the knowledge about foreign women is gleaned from Hollywood movies, and so many Chinese may assume you are provocative and 'easy'. In general, though, this leads to little more than staring; foreign women are unlikely to suffer sexual harassment here.

There have been a few reports of foreign women being hassled in parks or when walking or cycling at night; take a whistle or alarm with you. Beijing is very cosmopolitan, and shorts, tank tops and shorter skirts are worn by local women.

If you search, you'll find tampons in a few foreigner-friendly supermarkets but overall they're not readily available in China. It's also best to bring your own contraceptive pills.

Gay & Lesbian Travellers
While there is greater tolerance of homosexuality in Beijing than in China's more rural areas, it's not recommended that gays and lesbians be too open about their sexual orientation in public. Attitudes are changing, with an increasing number of gay singers and actors in China, but the police periodically crack down on gay meeting places. Gay clubs appear to function without official harassment, although they tend to be low profile. See p91 for gay and lesbian bars.

INFORMATION & ORGANISATIONS
The rarely updated 🖳 www .utopia-asia.com/tipschin.htm can provide some tips on travelling China, as well as listings of gay bars and clubs nationwide. You can also contact the International Gay and Lesbian Travel Association (☎ 1 954 776 2626; fax 776 3303; 🖳 www.iglta.com) in the USA or Club Exotika (🖳 www.clubexotika .com), which runs gay and lesbian tours to China.

Disabled Travellers
If you are wheelchair-bound or have a walking disability, Beijing will be a major obstacle course. Pavements are often crowded and in appalling condition, and high curbs prevent wheelchair access. Many streets can only be crossed via multistair underground walkways, and subways and buses are not accessible.

As wheelchairs are prohibitively expensive for most disabled people in China, attractions and buildings are not designed with access in mind. Those with sight, hearing or walking disabilities must be extremely cautious of traffic, which almost never yields to pedestrians. In this book, the ♿ symbol has been awarded only to places with ramps and lifts/elevators, and where wheelchairs can be manoeuvred.

INFORMATION & ORGANISATIONS

It can be useful to contact the travel officer of your national support organisation before leaving home; they can sometimes offer travel literature to help with planning and can put you in touch with appropriate tours. In the UK the Royal Association for Disability & Rehabilitation (12 City Forum, 250 City Rd, London EC1V 8AF; ☎ 020-7250 3222; fax 7250 0212; 🖳 radar@radar.org.uk) produces fact-packs for disabled travellers. In the USA try the Society for the Advancement of Travel for the Handicapped (SATH; Suite 601, 347 Fifth Ave, New York, NY 10016; ☎ 212-447 7284; 🖳 www.sath.org) and Access (PO Box 356, Malverne, CY 11565; ☎ 516-887 5798).

In France try the Comité National François de Liaison pour la Réadaptation des Handicapés (CNFLRH; 236 bis rue de Tolbiac, Paris; ☎ 01 53 80 66 66).

LANGUAGE

The official language of the People's Republic of China is Putonghua, based on (but not identical to) the Beijing Mandarin dialect and referred to as just plain Mandarin by most people. Mandarin dialects spoken in other regions of the country vary considerably.

Written Chinese script is based on ancient pictograph characters that have been simplified over time; while over 56,000 characters have been verified, it is commonly held that a well-educated Chinese person knows and uses between 6000 and 8000 characters. Pinyin has been developed as a romanisation of Mandarin using English letters, but many Beijingers cannot read it.

A growing number of Beijingers speak some English; in tourist hotels and restaurants and at major sights you'll get along OK without Mandarin. But if you venture into shops, neighbourhoods or conversations that are off the tourist track, you may find yourself lost for words. For a user-friendly guide, with pronunciation tips and a comprehensive phrase list (including script that you can simply show to people rather than speak), get a copy of Lonely Planet's *Mandarin phrasebook*.

Yuting Huaniao Shichang (Flower and Bird Market)

Index

EATING

SLEEPING

SHOPPING

Sights Index

24/7 travel advice

www.lonelyplanet.com